Mini Encyclopedia of

DOG
HEALTH

ROBERTA BAXTER
MA, VetMB, MRCVS

CONSULTANT: CHRIS C. PINNEY, DVM

First edition for the United States and Canada published in 2011 by Barron's Educational Series, Inc.

First published in 2010 by Interpet Publishing.
© Copyright 2010 by Interpet Publishing.

All inquiries should be addressed to:
Barron's Educational Series, Inc.
250 Wireless Boulevard
Hauppauge, NY 11788
www.barronseduc.com

ISBN-13: 978-0-7641-4550-6
ISBN-10: 0-7641-4550-9

Library of Congress Control Number: 2009932235

Printed in China
9 8 7 6 5 4 3 2 1

Printed and bound in China.

Author

Roberta Baxter, MA, VetMB, MRCVS, is a professional veterinarian with more than15 years experience. She has a particular interest in pain management in animals and is extremely enthusiastic about animal welfare, owner education, and preventative medicine. Roberta has written educational material for both horse and dog owners, as well as for veterinarians and support staff. She has also prepared articles for popular magazines and veterinary publications.

With thanks to Adam, Eddie, Stella for their help, and to my friends Jo, Elizabeth, and Jeanne for their advice as dog owners and veterinary professionals, respectively.

Consultant

Chris C. Pinney, DVM, is the author of eight books and has served as veterinary host and advisor for television news magazines and syndicated radio talk shows. He has set up a successful website to promote practical and affordable pet care (*www.veterinaryinsider.com*) and currently practices veterinary medicine in Houston, Texas.

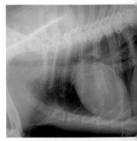

Part 1

How to have a healthy dog — 6–45

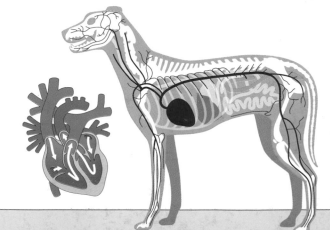

Part 2

Guide to health problems — 46–179

Contents

Part 3
First aid and emergencies
180–199

Contents

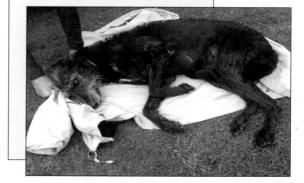

Part 1

How to have a healthy dog

Are you ready for a dog in your life? Have you thought about what having a dog will entail? Are you sure you have the time to take care of a dog properly? Taking care of a dog, whether an adult or puppy, is great fun and incredibly rewarding, but it is also a big responsibility. It can take up a great deal of time, money, and emotional energy, so it is best to consider such a step carefully. Talking to friends with dogs and spending some time with their pets, or maybe helping with dog-walking or caring for their pets when they are away will give you a chance to see how a dog might fit into your life. Think clearly about the constraints you have on your life already; your dog will have to fit around these. If you work full-time and there is no one at home during the day, a dog may not be for you. In addition to regular trips to the yard and at least one walk a day, dogs need grooming, feeding, training, and most importantly, plenty of love and attention.

The right kind and quantity of food is vital for good health.

Below: *A well-cared-for dog can be a great friend and companion. This Pomeranian needs regular grooming to keep its coat in good condition.*

Choosing the right dog

Should you be ready for a dog, your existing commitments to work, travel, family, and other pets may determine what kind of dog you should have. It is wise to choose the kind of dog that can fit into your life easily, so that both your family and the dog can enjoy each other's company to the fullest. Families with young children can offer plenty of love and attention to most types of dogs but are generally not ideal homes for the guarding breeds. These can be more inclined to aggressive and dominant behavior and do better on a one-on-one basis with an adult owner. Some breeds need more exercise and training than others and may be more likely to exhibit frustrated behavior if they are not exercised and trained

Left: Dachshunds can prove feisty but are great fun too.

Giant breeds such as Newfoundlands need plenty of time and attention.

Originally bred as gun dogs, Springer Spaniels also make great family pets.

sufficiently. Take some time to research the origins of the breed you are interested in and find out what level of care and attention it needs. This will help you to choose the right dog for you.

Puppy or mature dog?

Having a dog from puppyhood is great fun, but puppies need a great deal of care and attention, as well as a patient, consistent approach to training;

otherwise, they can become out of control. Only consider a puppy if someone is at home most of the time and can provide the puppy with what it needs. If this is not possible, a more mature dog may be a better option. Most dogs that are rehomed through rescue centers are there through no fault of their own. Either they were taken in by someone who had not considered what it would mean to keep a dog; or they have developed behavioral problems due to lack of exercise, training, and attention; or they are victims of a family breakdown. Offering a more mature dog a home may be the answer if you don't have the time for a puppy, but be aware – all dogs need plenty of attention!

Guarding breeds such as Rottweilers can be loyal pets, but their tendency toward dominant behavior may mean that they are not ideal for young families.

Above: *Greyhounds are generally easygoing, quiet, loyal characters – until they see a rabbit or a cat.*

Below: *Toy breeds, such as Chihuahuas, are easy to look after but can be nippy.*

Dalmatians are easy to care for but can be difficult to train.

What does your dog need?

From the smallest mini puppy to the oldest giant breed dog, all canines have the same basic set of needs. Considering their requirements carefully will help you keep them as happy and healthy as possible and will enable you to avoid health and behavioral problems.

Water All dogs should have constant access to a source of fresh water. Water should never be withdrawn, unless your veterinarian advises you to do so.

Food Dogs have basic nutritional requirements that differ markedly from ours, and these must be met if the animals are to remain healthy. Dogs are omnivores; ideally, their diet should incorporate meat and cereal products to provide sufficient protein, carbohydrates, and fat to meet their daily requirements. They also need sufficient amino acids, vitamins, minerals, and essential fatty acids to grow, maintain health, and heal from injury or disease.

Play is an essential part of dogs' lives. Provide appropriate toys.

Below: Stainless steel water and food bowls are ideal for most dogs and are available in a range of sizes.

Anti-bloat, or barrier bowls, help to slow down dogs if they eat too fast.

Shelter Like any animal, dogs need shelter from rain and snow and a warm, comfortable bedded area. In most cases this means providing a bed area in the home, but it is important that all outdoor dogs have access to a covered kennel area that is clean, dry, and insulated so that it is neither too warm nor too cold. Pay attention to drainage and the direction of prevailing winds to ensure that kennel areas are sheltered and do not flood. Shade in summer is also important to avoid overheating.

Exercise and access to the outdoors All dogs must have regular access to an area where they can relieve themselves. For most dogs this means letting them out into the yard at least every four hours during the day (more often for puppies), and not leaving them shut inside for more than eight hours at night. Leaving them longer than this may make it impossible for them to hold their bladders or bowels, resulting in accidents in the home. In addition, all dogs need a suitable level of exercise for their types and ages. This is best met by one or two walks or training sessions each day. During this time they need an opportunity to run around and stretch their legs, as well as have some fresh air and a change of scenery to avoid boredom.

Attention Dogs generally enjoy human interaction, as well as interaction with other dogs, and they benefit emotionally from play and attention. Grooming, petting, and checking dogs over regularly also allows owners to make sure there are no signs of disease or abnormalities that may need treatment or veterinary assessment.

Above: Plenty of human interaction helps make dogs happy. Owners get to know their dogs well and can recognize problems at an early stage.

What will I need?

Before bringing home your new pet, make sure you have the following items and equipment on hand:

A supply of the food that the dog is already accustomed to eating

Water and food bowls

A dog bed

A warm hot water bottle with a cover (if the puppy is a young one)

A collar and identity tag

A leash

Some toys

Healthy treats

An indoor crate to aid puppy training and house training. It will also help prevent the dog from chewing things it shouldn't.

Insurance for veterinary fees and also liability insurance (in case your dog inadvertently causes an accident or injury)

The weekly check

In order to take good care of your dog, it is important to be able to recognize any problems that may occur. Some diseases may cause overt symptoms, such as vomiting, diarrhea, lameness, coughing, or panting, but others are more subtle and will only be picked up in the early stages by a vigilant owner. Petting, stroking, and play all help you and your dog to bond, but it is helpful to set aside some special time each week to check over your dog and teach him to tolerate being examined. This will stand him in good stead when he does need to go to the groomer or veterinarian, or when you need to give him medicines or apply treatments. Giving your dog a series of commands to associate with different areas being checked, such as "stay,

teeth, eyes, feet" and so on allows him to learn what to expect. Make it fun and use plenty of praise and treats to build his confidence, but be thorough, too.

What to look for

Carrying out the following checks will alert you to any changes in your dog's normal appearance. Any signs of disease or abnormality can then be checked out promptly by your veterinarian.

Above and left: Start by stroking your dog all over and getting used to the feel of his fur, as well as its thickness, and the appearance of the skin beneath. Feel the head and neck, all over the trunk and tummy, all four limbs, and the tail.

Below: Try to feel deeper so that you can recognize any swellings within or under the skin. Make a note of any lumps or bumps that you discover, and cut some hair nearby so that you can find them again when you get them checked out by the veterinarian.

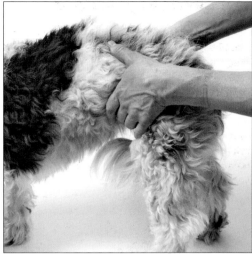

Above: Slide your hands down your dog's back to make sure there are no tender areas.

Left, right, and below: Gently lift each limb one by one off the ground and move it back and forth to check that it is comfortable. Examine the paws carefully for grass seeds and splinters. Make sure the nails are neither overgrown nor too short, as this can indicate scuffing due to mobility problems.

Left: Ask your dog to sit and stay and have a good look at his face. Start with his ears; feel down the ear flaps and around behind them, then lift them up and look into his ears. They should be clean and should not smell. The presence of a discharge or of excessive wax could indicate a problem that may need attention.

Below: The eyes should be wide open and appear bright and clear, with no discharge or excessive production of tears.

Above: Check the nose for signs of discharge, and make sure the skin is soft and supple and not cracked or sore.

Below and right: *Lift the lips and check the teeth. Open the mouth and make sure the tongue appears normal.*

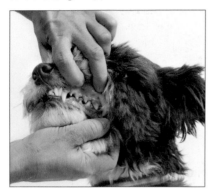

Below: *Finally, make sure your pooch enjoys his check; make a big fuss of him and give him a healthy treat.*

15

Clipping nails, bathing, and checking anal sacs

Like us, dogs develop with the basic architecture for five toes on each foot. However, the dewclaw (the thumb or big toe) does not always develop and is sometimes removed, which means that dogs may have four or five toes on each foot. It is important to check whether or not they have a dewclaw (which also needs clipping), as it is easy to miss and may become overgrown. The nails contain a quick, which has a good blood supply and will bleed a lot if nails are clipped too short. Be careful when clipping and ask your veterinarian or groomer to show you what to do if you are worried.

Nails that are not worn down by regular pavement exercise may need regular trimming.

Use strong, sharp nail clippers.

Nail cutting

Left: *Hold the paw steady and support the nail so that you can clip it accurately without damaging the quick.*

Within the nail, the quick has a high blood supply and bleeds copiously if damaged.

Right: *The dewclaws are found on the side of the leg. Trim off the sharp tip of each nail, leaving a healthy shorter nail that is less likely to become damaged.*

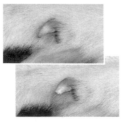

Overgrown nails

Overgrown nails can interfere with the normal position of the toes and can cause them to become painful. Cut off the nails 2–3 mm below the quick (if it is visible) or parallel with the base of the pad if the nail is opaque.

Bathing

Bathing dogs too frequently or with strong deodorizing shampoos can strip the natural oils out of the coat and contribute to dry, rough skin and a predisposition to skin irritation. You can use gentle baby shampoos or hypoallergenic dog shampoos, but it is best to avoid shampooing dogs more than once a month, unless a skin problem necessitates more frequent bathing with a medicated shampoo.

Having your dog bathed and clipped by a qualified groomer is the easiest option, but if you want to bathe him at home, be sure to use a nonslip mat in the bath or shampoo him outside in the yard on a sunny day, with the hose connected to a warm water source.

The anal sacs

Scent glands located in the anal sacs under a dog's tail, in the vicinity of the anus, can cause irritation (exhibited as licking and scooting on the bottom) and can result in a nasty smell. If blocked, anal sacs may need to be squeezed and emptied by a veterinarian or experienced groomer.

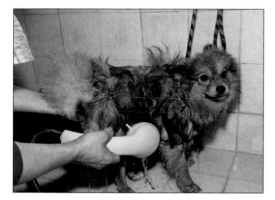

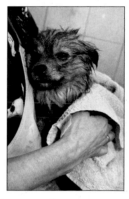

1. An occasional bath is good for the coat and helps keep doggy smells to a minimum. Use a shower spray and comfortably warm water.

2. Always use a gentle shampoo to avoid causing skin irritation.

3. Be sure to dry the dog thoroughly to prevent chilling.

4. Thorough grooming helps to remove dead hairs and maintain healthy skin. Use the correct type of grooming brush for dogs with long coats.

Anal sacs

Anal sac blockage can cause .... itchiness and skin irritation.

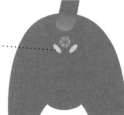

Dental care

Check your dog's teeth to make sure they are clean and white and not covered in a scale of tartar. Also examine the nearby gums – reddening or bleeding can indicate an infection called gingivitis. Keep the teeth and gums healthy by cleaning them twice a week; otherwise, dental disease can lead to mouth pain, loss of appetite, and digestive problems. It can also cause infections that spread from the gums via the bloodstream to affect the heart and other organs.

Tooth development

A pup's mouth normally contains 28 deciduous, or milk, teeth, which are replaced by 44 adult teeth between around three and seven months of age. However, in some individuals, deciduous baby teeth are not shed normally, even though adult teeth develop right next to them. This can lead to damage of the mature teeth, so any retained milk teeth may need surgical removal. Also, any dogs whose teeth do not meet properly (a common feature of a number of breeds due to their face shape) may be predisposed to dental problems.

Above: *A thorough examination of the teeth should be carried out regularly to allow any problems to be identified and treated.*

Above: *Despite the arrival of an adult canine tooth, the deciduous tooth has not been lost. Surgical removal prevents damage to the adult tooth.*

Stone chewing

Some dogs obsessively chew stones, and for them, tooth chipping or breaking is a common problem, and swallowed stones can cause stomach and intestinal disease (see pages 76–77). Prevent access to graveled areas of yards or use a gentle muzzle to stop dogs from picking up stones. Damaged teeth may require removal or filling.

Bones and hard chews help to keep the teeth clean.

Plaque and tartar

During eating, food particles and bacteria in the mouth cause plaque and tartar to be deposited on the teeth. In the wild, chewing bones would reduce tartar buildup, but our dogs have a healthier, if softer, diet that does not keep the teeth so clean. A number of different approaches can be used to slow tartar buildup. If plaque does develop on the teeth, dental descaling and polishing may become necessary, which both require a general anesthetic.

Preventing plaque

- *Carry out twice-weekly cleaning.*

- *Provide regular dental chews or bones (for those dogs that can tolerate them).*

- *Some dogs benefit from oral antiseptics in drinking water.*

How to clean a dog's teeth

Aim to clean the teeth at least twice weekly.

1. Start gradually. Accustom the dog to having his face stroked and his lips and mouth handled.

2. Progress slowly until you are able to run your finger over all his teeth.

3. Try introducing a finger brush or a canine toothbrush and finally toothpaste. Do not use human minty toothpaste; a doggy version (poultry- or malt-flavored) is much more palatable and will cause less dribbling.

4. Gently work your way in small circles methodically around the mouth.

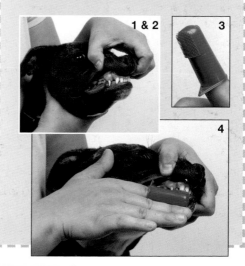

1 & 2   3   4

Vaccination, worming, giving tablets

Vaccines can provide dogs with immunity against a number of serious infectious diseases. They not only protect individual dogs against these conditions—they also help reduce the prevalence of them in a community of dogs. Protecting dogs also helps prevent them from being a source of infection for their owners, as some of these diseases are zoonotic (transmissible to humans).

Vaccines

A number of different vaccines are available for dogs. Choosing which are appropriate may depend on where in the world you live and thus what infections your dog may come into contact with in that area.

In the U.S., Europe, and the U.K., vaccines are available that provide dogs with immunity against distemper, adenoviral hepatitis, parvovirus, parainfluenza virus, and leptospirosis. Some vaccination protocols also include coronavirus. In certain parts of the world the Lyme disease vaccination is also available. In addition, rabies vaccines are used to protect dogs living in countries such as the U.S. and continental Europe, where rabies is prevalent in the wild animal population. It can also be given to dogs in rabies-free

Above: *Out on walks, a dog can come into contact with infectious diseases and worms. Make sure all his treatments and vaccinations are up to date.*

countries, such as the U.K., as part of their preparation for traveling abroad. Kennel cough vaccination is also commonly given before travel, kenneling, and other situations where dogs are mixed or stressed and have an increased chance of coming into contact with this highly infectious disease.

Local requirements

In the U.S., puppies are vaccinated against distemper, hepatitis, parvovirus, parainfluenza virus, and, optionally, leptospirosis. They usually have their first vaccine at eight weeks of age and their second three weeks later. Other vaccines may be given on an "as required" basis.

When to give vaccines

Vaccination protocols depend on the data sheet recommendations of the vaccine manufacturers, but as a general principle most puppies are given preliminary vaccines at around the time when they leave their mother and go to their new home, with a follow-up vaccine two to four weeks later. They traditionally require a yearly booster vaccine for most diseases, although some components give immunity for more than a year and may only need boosting every two to three years. Keeping good records and showing these to the veterinarian when you take your dog for vaccinations allows the veterinarian to work out exactly which vaccines your dog needs.

Worming

Dogs need regular deworming treatments to protect them against worms and other intestinal parasites. Common problems include tapeworms, roundworms, heartworm, lungworms, and hookworms, some of which may also be transmissible to children and adults who are in contact with the infected dog.

Most puppies need worming every month with a combined wormer that has broad-spectrum efficacy. Adult dogs may usually be wormed less frequently, although monthly worming may still be necessary in some high-risk areas of the world.

Giving a vaccination

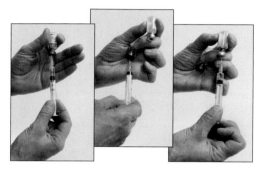

Above: The veterinarian mixes and prepares appropriate vaccines for injection. Keep clear records of your dog's vaccinations to help your veterinarian.

Above: The veterinarian will hold the dog firmly and clean the skin on the back of the neck at the site of injection. The dog should remain calm at this point.

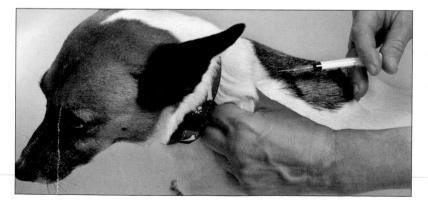

Left: The vaccine is injected under the skin. This is not painful and most dogs tolerate injections well.

Pregnant females should be wormed before their pregnancy starts and then according to the worming manufacturer's guidelines.

Ectoparasites

Many dogs also need regular monthly flea treatments, most effectively administered as spot-on medicines. Some are also effective against lice and mange. In tick areas, it may also be necessary to use products with anti-tick efficacy, as ticks can transmit Lyme disease and other bacterial infections, including babesiosis and ehrlichiosis.

Heartworm is a major concern in the U.S. as well. Therefore, your dog should be routinely checked for this condition, as it can lead to very serious health problems if not treated immediately and effectively.

Below: Antiparasitic treatments help to keep dogs healthy and are not difficult to apply.

Applying a spot-on flea treatment

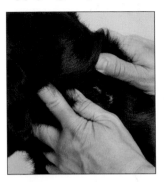

Left: First, part the hair on the back of the neck so that you can see the skin.

Left: Following the instructions, apply the spot-on antiparasitic treatment directly to the skin.

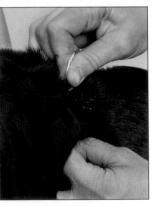

Left: The treatment takes a little while to soak in, so avoid touching the area for a few hours.

How to give tablets

Many dogs will take tablets in food; check with your veterinarian that the tablets can be given with food. If so, mix them in something really tasty, such as a little wet food, or wrap them up in ham or cheese if your dog can tolerate these.

Try throwing the tablets to your dog; if he is accustomed to catching and swallowing treats, he may do the same with medicines.

Alternatively, open your dog's mouth wide, place the tablets on his tongue as far down his throat as you can without being bitten, hold his mouth closed, and stroke his throat until he swallows.

Giving tablets

Left: To encourage a dog to accept medication, try offering treats with the tablets. Dogs will gradually become accustomed to the routine.

Above: Placing a tablet on the back of the tongue activates a swallowing reflex.

Above: Hold the dog's mouth closed and stroke the throat while the dog swallows.

23

Traveling with your dog

A number of dangers can be associated with travel. Any kind of traffic accident can result in injuries if animals are not adequately restrained, so it is important to make pets safe during travel.

Basic precautions

Buy a harness with a seat belt loop that will steady the dog on the back seat of a car. Make sure it fits appropriately and is adequately adjusted or it could cause, rather than prevent, injuries. Alternatively, transport your dog in the rear section of the car in a crate or with a barrier up, so that he cannot fly forward in the event of an accident. Use an indoor crate for travel via airplane.

During journeys, make sure your dog does not overheat. Try to provide him with a shady area and make sure there is good air flow on hot days. Aim to stop every two hours to offer him water and the opportunity to relieve himself, and avoid feeding him if he shows signs of travel sickness.

Above: A harness or canine seat belt helps keep dogs safe during car travel. Practice fitting the harness in advance of your journey.

Health certificates and export certificates

Travel within the U.S. requires health certificates. These state that the dog has no signs of infectious disease and may be valid for up to ten days. Export certificates and import licenses are usually required for international travel. Check with the United States Department of Agriculture (USDA).

Dogs are particularly vulnerable to getting lost or to straying when traveling, especially if they are not familiar with the route. So, during rest stops, be sure to keep your dog close to you and on a leash.

Microchipping

A microchip is a small device that carries an individual number or a collection of numbers and letters. It is implanted under the skin, usually on the back of the neck between the shoulder blades, and enables an individual dog to be identified using a handheld scanner. Microchipping offers a mechanism for providing dogs with a source of identification that can be used to reunite them with their owners should

Pet passports

Pet passports allow pets to travel internationally without having to remain in quarantine on their arrival in a number of rabies-free countries, such as the U.K. To qualify, dogs must be permanently identified with a microchip and have been vaccinated against rabies. To use the Pet Travel Scheme to move between rabies-free countries, they must also have had a blood test to prove that they developed adequate immunity from the vaccination. Further criteria include proof of certain worming and antiparasitic treatments. Details vary among countries and are available from government departments dealing with the import and export of animals.

they stray or become lost. It can also be a useful means of proving a dog is yours if he is stolen. Various microchips can be used and not all are international, so it is important to make sure that your pet carries a valid microchip that will work in each country you take him to, and that his details are entered on the relevant national database(s).

International travel

Dogs that travel internationally may move through countries where infections exist against which they have no natural immunity. This means that they may need even more protection than local dogs. Dogs are also particularly prone to picking up insect-borne infections

in hot and damp climates, especially if that is not their natural habitat. Research appropriate antiparasitic treatments before entering an area so that you can provide dogs with as much protection against such diseases as possible. This may necessitate particular spot-on treatments or antiparasitic collars. In addition, dogs that are not already vaccinated against rabies should be inoculated before travel into rabies-endemic areas.

Dealing with car travel sickness

Dogs that experience travel sickness may do so because they are anxious about traveling or find the movement difficult to cope with. Sedation can help calm dogs for long journeys but can be dangerous if they have underlying heart or breathing problems or if it is particularly hot. Herbal calming tablets work successfully in some cases. However, most dogs cope better if they are gradually allowed to get used to being in the car when it is stationary for feeding and play. Introduce engine noise and short trips at a later date. It may also be worth experimenting with the dog's traveling position in the car. Some dogs cope better if they are down on the floor; others do better up on the seat with a good view.

Feeding your dog

Feeding your dog an appropriate diet is central to his healthy development and growth and will give him the best chance of a long and happy life.

A healthy diet must incorporate a sufficient level of the main nutrients in a form that your dog can digest. Any nutrients in excess of requirements are lost in the feces, but providing an excessive level of some can cause problems, as can a deficiency of others.

Excessive levels of food can contribute to obesity, an increasing problem that may soon affect as many as half our dogs, contributing to heart disease, breathing problems, orthopedic conditions, and diabetes. Obese dogs are more likely to suffer pain and distress due to disease and may have shorter lives.

Choosing the best diet

The digestive system converts food into energy and essential nutrients in a complicated multistage process.

Some dogs do best on a combination of canned dog food and mixer.

Others prefer a complete dry kibble diet.

Home-cooked diets work well in some cases.

Healthy mouths

At least a portion of your dog's diet should be dry food, as chewing this helps to keep the teeth clean and healthy. Bones and chews can also help maintain a healthy mouth.

Digestion starts in the mouth, with chewing and salivary enzymes; it continues in the stomach, which holds the food and mixes it with more enzymes to break down particles, and is then followed by absorption of nutrients and water from the small and large intestines.

Problems at any stage can interfere with the process of food breakdown and absorption. Each food type is digested in a slightly different way, and one type may suit an individual dog more than another. In order to provide a balanced diet, you have several feeding options. (Fresh water should always be available.)

A dry kibble diet This is formulated to contain balanced levels of nutrients and is the most straightforward way to feed dogs.

A mixed diet A mixture of moist, meat-based food and an appropriate quantity of kibble to provide the required balance of nutrients.

A home-cooked diet Raw or cooked meat, vegetables, and carbohydrate sources, as well as vitamin and mineral supplements. Some advocates believe that such foods are less likely to be associated with a variety of diseases. However, providing the right

Right: Feeding a healthy diet that your dog enjoys is central to his well-being. There is a wide choice of foods available, some formulated specially for puppies or older dogs.

balance of nutrients can be difficult, and associated health problems can result. Also, feeding raw meat has been associated with gastrointestinal infections such as *Salmonella*.

Essential nutrients

A dog needs sufficient energy levels for his lifestyle, but not excessive calories, otherwise he will become overweight. Energy can be provided as carbohydrate and/or fat. Protein and its constituent amino acids are required for growth, healing injuries, and biological processes within the body.

The diet must include minerals such as calcium, phosphorus, sodium, chloride, and magnesium, as well as trace elements such as iron, copper, manganese, zinc, iodine, selenium, and cobalt. These minerals

Change diets gradually

Any changes in diet should be made gradually over a period of five to seven days to prevent diarrhea and vomiting due to digestive disturbances.

act as building blocks for bone and other cell types; maintain healthy skin, muscle, and kidneys; and are necessary for red blood cell production and the formation of thyroid hormones. Some also have a role in helping prevent cancer and slowing the signs of aging.

Vitamins are also needed for growth, development, and the maintenance of a healthy body. Some are fat-soluble and are only derived from fat in the diet, so some fat is needed. Others are water-soluble and are found in plant matter. These are added into compounded foods.

Feeding puppies

A young puppy is growing and developing fast and needs higher levels of nutrients than an adult. To achieve this, provide four meals a day at first. This is generally reduced to three meals daily at around four months of age, two meals daily at six to nine months, and then sometimes one meal daily.

By the age of six months, the puppy should be around 50% of its adult weight. It is important to avoid over-fast growth as this can be associated with an increased incidence of bone and joint problems. Also, fat cells laid down at this age can predispose your puppy to obesity later in life, so try to prevent puppies from becoming overweight.

Food formulated for puppies contains higher levels of protein, energy, and minerals, which can help reduce joint problems. It is particularly important to modulate the levels of calcium and phosphorus to allow optimum growth. Feeding too much of either interferes with the other, so offer a good-quality puppy food, as this will contain adequate nutrient levels. Do not give any calcium supplements.

Feeding adult dogs

Adult dogs that are no longer in their growth phase have lower nutrient requirements. Keep a close eye on their feeding to prevent obesity as they mature. Provide a high-quality maintenance food and avoid vitamin and mineral supplements; abnormal mineral levels can cause problems. Dogs with a tendency to gain weight should be offered a lower-calorie food to help control their size.

Feeding during pregnancy and lactation

During pregnancy and lactation, female dogs require the same kind of nutrient balance as puppies, so increase their feeding levels according to demand from the dog. As a general rule, increase the food intake by 15% each week from week five of pregnancy.

Above: Older dogs may have specific dietary requirements. Take care not to overfeed them.

Continue to increase this intake during lactation, as a female dog feeding four- or five-week-old puppies will need around three times her normal nutrient intake. Feeding a female on puppy food in several meals daily will help her to take in sufficient nutrient levels and keep pace with the demands of her growing puppies without becoming underweight or suffering dangerously low nutrient levels herself.

Feeding geriatric pets

Geriatric pets are often less mobile and excitable and so have lower metabolic rates and less energy requirements. Giant-breed dogs age fastest, and giant breeds over six years of age benefit from the lower levels of energy, fat, and salt and the higher proportion of fiber that senior foods have to offer. Increased levels of fiber also help combat constipation, a common

Diarrhea and vomiting

In addition to veterinary treatment, dogs with vomiting and diarrhea due to gastroenteritis may benefit from twelve to twenty-four hours of fasting, followed by a bland, easily digestible diet. This could be a low-allergy or sensitivity food or cooked, deboned chicken and rice in a ration of one-third chicken to two-thirds rice. Start by offering several small meals throughout the day and then gradually wean the dog back to normal mealtimes. Then gradually reintroduce the dog's normal food. Water should always be available and electrolyte solutions may also be needed to help prevent dehydration.

problem in older dogs. Medium- to large-sized dogs over eight years old similarly benefit from senior foods, as do small breeds over about ten years of age.

Feeding senior foods helps prevent obesity and reduces constipation. It also helps control early signs of aging, such as increased drinking and muscle loss, by reducing the workload of essential organs such as the liver and kidneys.

Feeding for disease

Dogs with specific diseases can be given special prescription foods that help treat the disease in question by manipulating the diet. Although there are recipes to home-cook such foods, it is easiest to use proprietary foods available from veterinarians. Certain nutritional supplements can also be helpful in the treatment of specific diseases.

Weight problems

It only takes a 1% calorie excess over a period of time to gain weight, but calorie intake needs to be reduced to around 65% of the previous food level to allow weight loss. This can be achieved by reducing the amount fed (especially treats) or by moving onto a low-calorie food. Your veterinarian may even prescribe an ultra-low-calorie food temporarily to aid weight loss. An increase in exercise will also help shift excess fat.

By contrast, inadequate levels of food or inappropriate food can contribute to low body weight, weakness, poor muscling, skin diseases, bone disorders, heart and lung problems, and a poor immune system. Diarrhea and vomiting may also be seen, and liver and kidney problems can result.

Being overweight ⋯⋯ predisposes dogs to a range of problems.

Slender dogs are ⋯⋯ likely to remain healthier.

Training and exercise

Puppies enjoy learning new tricks and skills. Early training allows owners to capitalize on their pet's receptive and confident mind to establish good behavior from the first. Young puppies learn far more quickly than older dogs, and puppies under the age of four to five months have not yet established a fear response, reacting to new environments with confidence and interest. This means that young puppies should be taken out and about, introduced to other animals, traffic, rides in the car, and other people and children as early as possible. Dogs socialized early tend to be far less fearful and less likely to develop phobias than puppies kept in for longer. Although this has to be weighed against the importance of vaccinations to protect puppies in new environments, early vaccinations allow puppies to be out by eleven to twelve weeks of age. Puppy socialization classes generally start even earlier, as they often only require puppies to have had their first vaccination.

Above: Early socialization helps dogs develop positive and confident behavior.

First steps

From the first day you bring your puppy home, you can take him out and about (albeit in your arms if he is not yet vaccinated) and allow him to experience as much as possible. Until he has had his complete set of vaccinations and they have had time to work (usually one to two weeks after the final vaccination), he is still susceptible to disease. Restrict him to the house and an enclosed yard that is not accessible to unvaccinated dogs. Do not allow him down on the ground elsewhere.

It is a good idea to get a collar on him immediately and to start heel and leash training in the yard, so that he quickly becomes accustomed to wearing a collar and walking to heel and on the leash.

Basic commands

You can also teach him some basic commands and encourage him to follow them, but all teaching should be positive (by encouragement and rewards).

Clicker training

A clicker is one of the best aids to training. Use it to help reward your dog for good behavior and following instructions. Training your dog to associate a "click" from a dog clicker with a positive reward (such as a treat or toy) can, over time, allow the click itself to become the reward. Easy to activate quickly and at exactly the right moment to reinforce good behavior, the clicker can provide a more immediate reward than food or treats, and can be used in conjunction with other methods to assist training.

Shouting and hitting do not work so well and can cause puppies to become fearful, which makes it harder for them to learn. Eye contact is essential when training dogs. Bear in mind that puppies have a short attention span; do not do too much at a time so they become bored. Instead, incorporate a few minutes of training into play every now and again.

Learning to "stay" is more complex and takes more practice.

Sit
Push the puppy's bottom into a sitting position, say the word "sit" calmly but firmly, and reward your dog with petting or a treat when he achieves it.

Down
Place your dog in the down position flat on the floor, say "down," and reward him.

Stand
Put your dog in a standing position, say the command, and reward him.

Above: *Learning to "sit" for a treat or before being fed is quickly mastered.*

The command "stand" can also be rewarded.

Stay
Ask your dog to sit and then say "Stay." Back off with your hand up and call him to you quickly so that he is rewarded for not coming until you call. Gradually extend the period for which you ask him to "Stay."

Come
Call your dog to you with your arms open wide. Treat and reward him when he arrives.

Advanced commands
It can also be helpful to teach commands during the weekly check-over. This can help your dog when you need to examine

him or take him to the veterinarian. Teaching him the commands will help him learn what to expect.

Above: *Teaching the "paw" command makes examining paws much easier if lameness develops at a later date.*

Teeth
Lift his lip and examine his teeth. Use this command when you clean them too.

Eyes
Use this when you are checking his eyes.

Paws
Give him this command when you are checking each paw.

Further advanced commands can be incorporated into training sessions. It can be helpful to introduce whistle and hand commands when training "sit," "stay," and "come" commands, as dogs can respond to a whistle over a greater distance and can often hear a whistle even when they are becoming deaf. Choosing a consistent tone for each command and giving the whistle command together with verbal and hand commands helps strengthen your dog's response.

Training is a matter of giving your dog a consistent signal and rewarding his response to it with plenty of attention and some healthy treats. Simply ignore inappropriate responses; dogs soon learn when they are rewarded for getting something right.

House training
With positive training methods, puppies quickly learn to be clean in the house. As soon as your young puppy arrives home, take him out into the yard for frequent toilet trips. Reward any toileting done in the correct place with plenty of attention and praise. Ignore and quietly clean up accidents in the house. House training can take weeks or months to complete, but with a patient approach and regular, two-hourly trips out, puppies can learn to control themselves in the house and eventually can be left for four hours or so at a time.

Aids to house training include placing incontinence pads or newspaper near the door for puppies to use if they need to go and cannot get out. Encourage the puppies to use the paper and reward them for doing so. Gradually move the paper toward the door and out into the yard as puppies get the hang of using it.

Using a crate generally works best. Dogs will not readily soil their sleeping areas, so making a bed area inside that a dog is happy to use creates a place that the dog will try to keep clean at all costs. Confining him to the crate at night or when you are out encourages him to wait to be allowed out

Above: *Using an indoor crate allows your puppy to have a comfy bed in a safe place that he knows is his. It also helps prevent house damage and aids house training, as puppies generally avoid soiling their crate.*

Above: Toys packed with food help keep dogs stimulated and reduce the chance of destructive behavior arising from boredom.

before toileting. If dogs persistently soil the house at a particular time of day when the owner is out, it may be necessary to alter their feeding time so that their "need to go" coincides better with their exercise routine.

Chewing

All puppies need to chew when their teeth are coming in, as it helps stimulate the gums and make them more comfortable. Provide puppies with plenty of chewy toys and rawhide chews. When they pick up your things, take them away with a firm "No" and give them one of their own toys instead. In time – and as long as they have sufficient stimulation in their lives – they will learn to chew their own things and leave yours alone.

Dogs that become destructive generally do so out of boredom and lack of stimulation. They often need more exercise and training to give them other things to think about. They may also benefit from interactive toys, such as puzzle feeders. These release food slowly as they are played with and can occupy dogs for hours.

Confining dogs to an indoor crate while you are out can prevent them from destroying your belongings, but they need plenty of toys and space within the crate.

Keep a close eye on what your dog is chewing and remove it if it starts to become damaged or if any small parts could break off. Broken toys, chews, pieces of bone, and stones are all common causes of gut damage or blockage if swallowed, and can result in dogs needing an emergency operation.

Exercise

Exercise fulfills a number of important roles in your dog's life. It helps keep his bones and muscles strong, maintains heart function and strength, and keeps the lungs healthy. It stimulates the immune system and assists in preventing dogs from becoming overweight. In addition, exercise plays a very important

Below: Where possible, take your dog for two to three walks daily, building up, depending on breed and type of dog, from five to ten minutes per walk at twelve weeks of age to around thirty to sixty minutes per walk by twelve months.

role in both your dog's quality of life and your own. It helps keep your dog happy and allows him to experience new sights and sounds and meet other dogs, all of which help to prevent boredom. That in turn enables him to relax when at home and to be far less likely to develop behavioral problems or become destructive.

Most dogs benefit from two or three walks or exercise periods a day, in addition to free time in the yard. The appropriate type and amount of exercise varies from one dog to another, depending on their age, health status, and breed. However, it is great for both owner and dog to get into the habit of going out at least twice daily right from the start. Keeping exercise levels fairly consistent on a day-to-day basis helps prevent the kinds of injuries that can occur when dogs exercise beyond their capabilities.

Exercising puppies

Young, vaccinated puppies can be taken for a ten- to fifteen-minute walk down the road or to the park. As they mature, gradually build up to a longer walk. Include periods of off-leash play and retrieving to increase the speed of exercise. Training "sit," "stay," and "come" can also make walks more fun and help exercise the brain, too.

Do not exercise young dogs too much, even if they appear to enjoy it. Avoid taking them for long runs or endurance walks until their bones and joints are mature. This can take from eighteen months of age for large breed dogs, such as Rottweilers, Labrador Retrievers, and German Shepherd Dogs, to two years for giant breed dogs, such as Great Danes and Mastiffs. Too much exercise too soon can contribute to the development of bone and joint diseases.

Exercising adult dogs

As dogs enter adulthood they can enjoy more rigorous forms of exercise, as long as they have no underlying

Above: *Even in winter and bad weather, regular exercise is important, especially for active breeds of working dogs, such as this Finnish Spitz.*

joint or limb problems. Walks can gradually become longer and faster, with more time off the leash. Agile breeds may be taken running and for longer, endurance-style walks. Sports such as Cani-cross (cross-country running with dogs) and hill-walking may be appropriate. Build up exercise levels gradually, as dogs – like their owners – need to increase fitness progressively, conditioning joints and bones to the increased levels of workload and stress.

Other exciting forms of exercise include agility, flyball, and gundog training, all of which can be done at local clubs. In common with training classes, they offer you and your dog the opportunity to socialize and have some fun, too.

An awareness of the history of your dog's breed can help you choose the kinds of exercise he will like best and find easiest. Labradors and other retrievers generally enjoy retrieving but can be a little bulky for agility and flyball, which are more appropriate for terrier and collie types. Similarly, Huskies and hound breeds can make good running partners, while the heavier, guarding breeds, such as Rottweilers and Mastiffs, may cope better with slower and more grounded types of exercise. There are exceptions to every rule, and individual dogs may love to do sports that they are ill-suited to by their body shape; encouraging them may increase their chances of injury.

Exercise for senior dogs

Older dogs – giant breeds over the age of six and small breeds over the age of ten – may have specific exercise requirements. As they grow older their mobility levels often deteriorate due to injuries, joint aging, and arthritic changes in their joints. In addition, other diseases such as heart conditions, breathing problems, and hormonal conditions, may affect their ability to cope with exercise. As they grow older still, they may start to experience problems with balance, vision, and

hearing and become more confused, which may affect what kinds of exercise they can enjoy.

Older dogs also have lower calorie requirements which, if not taken into account and combined with a reduction in exercise levels, can contribute to obesity. This in turn makes it harder for joints to function and the heart and lungs to cope with exercise.

As dogs age, therefore, it is important to keep an eye on their exercise levels and feeding. Avoid obesity by reducing food levels and offering senior foods, which generally have lower calorie levels. Maintain exercise levels as much as possible to keep dogs mobile. Fresh water should always be available, particularly before and after exercise, and during exercise of any length, especially on a hot day.

Dogs with mobility problems will benefit from consistent levels of exercise on a day-to-day basis. Aim for three short walks every day and do not go for a three-mile hike on the weekend if your dog does not normally have that level of exercise. Try to encourage

Below: Fit, healthy adult dogs can build up their endurance and enjoy sports such as hill-walking. Waterproof coats for dogs may be necessary.

Above: Older dogs still enjoy varied exercise, as long as it is within their ability and does not cause exhaustion or lameness.

your dog to go out regularly, but do not push him to go faster or further than he can manage; otherwise an injury may result. Hydrotherapy may provide a useful means of continuing exercise and maintaining limb strength in such dogs, as it allows for joint movement and muscle fitness without full weight bearing on old limbs.

Dogs with heart or lung problems may pant or cough during exercise, and this may limit their ability to exercise. Always seek veterinary attention if any symptoms of this kind occur. Again, be guided by your dog and do not push him too hard. Exercise dogs in the early morning and evening, avoiding the heat of the day, when exercise will be particularly difficult.

In order to prevent accidents and injuries, keep an extra careful eye on dogs that are going blind or deaf or are becoming confused. Blind dogs may exercise off the leash with a sighted companion, as they will often follow another dog, particularly if it wears a bell on its collar. Avoid off-leash exercise near roads, water, and other dangers. Exercise on an extending leash may be far more appropriate and safe for blind or deaf dogs.

Injuries and convalescence

When dogs suffer bone or joint injuries, they may need to be rested or undergo convalescent exercise regimens to rebuild strength. Bear in mind the following points:

• Any injury that results in a sudden onset of lameness may involve the joints and should be treated with rest, pending an urgent veterinary checkup.

• Should a joint problem be suspected, the veterinarian will probably advise a period of strict rest to allow healing. This will generally involve house rest, with only brief, controlled (i.e., on-leash) trips to the yard for your dog to relieve himself. In some cases, a five- to ten-minute leash walk twice daily may also be appropriate.

• As injuries heal, gradually increase the level of exercise over a two- to four-week period until normal exercise levels are resumed. Too sudden an increase in exercise risks recurrence of the injury.

• Dogs that have had surgery may require a longer period of convalescence. Depending on the injury and the type of surgery, exercise may involve five minutes of leash walking twice daily at first, building up over a month to ten to fifteen minutes twice daily. Further increases may follow as strength develops.

• Specific physiotherapy exercises can help to increase strength in particular parts of the body. Dogs may be walked on and off the pavement curb or over poles to increase their coordination and ability to strengthen their limbs. Other exercises may strengthen particular muscle groups. A veterinarian or physiotherapist may prescribe an appropriate exercise plan.

• Hydrotherapy may also aid recovery from injuries or assist the development of strength in dogs with underlying problems such as hip dysplasia (see page 172). Controlled swimming against water jets in a canine hydrotherapy pool or work on an underwater treadmill in varying levels of water can strengthen core muscles and improve joint strength and mobility.

Below: *Hydrotherapy can be a great benefit to many dogs. The level and duration of swimming can be built up gradually in a pool to increase fitness and strength and aid recovery from injuries.*

Above: *An X-ray of an immature dog with open growth plates that make his limbs particularly vulnerable to damage due to inappropriate exercise or injuries.*

Neutering

Most dogs that are not intended for breeding are neutered at around six to nine months of age. This not only avoids the conception of unwanted puppies, but it can also have health benefits for the dogs themselves.

Neutering involves removing the sex glands – the testicles in a male dog and the ovaries, usually with part of the uterus, in the female.

The benefits of neutering

In male dogs, neutering helps to prevent straying and inappropriate sexual behavior and can help prevent aggressiveness and dominance. Prostate disease is a common problem in older males that are not castrated. Testicular tumors can also occur in old male dogs but can also be avoided by prior castration. Even in young dogs, undescended testicles are prone to developing tumors, so castration is particularly important for those dogs whose testicles do not descend naturally by six to nine months of age.

For females there are even more health benefits. Every season (estrus) experienced by a female dog involves a surge of hormones that significantly increase her chance of developing breast cancer later in life. A female dog spayed before her first season has a very small chance of developing tumors in her mammary

tissue, while around a quarter of unspayed mature female dogs will develop mammary masses.

Older unspayed female dogs are also prone to developing pyometra, a nasty uterine infection that generally necessitates an emergency operation to remove the uterus. Spaying obviously prevents this life-threatening condition. In addition, female dogs that are diabetic or epileptic tend to cope better and have fewer problems if they are spayed. However, it is thought that spaying can result in female dogs being more likely to experience urinary incontinence later in life, although this is not a common problem and is usually treatable when it does occur.

When to neuter

While the timing is not an issue for males, who can be castrated safely at around six to nine months or later,

Neutering females

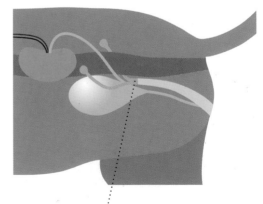

Both ovaries and horns and body of the uterus are normally removed, leaving part of the vagina within.

Chemical neutering

Though not commonly done in the U.S., temporary neutering can be achieved using medicines that inhibit testosterone in the male. These can reduce libido and help treat prostate disorders. Medicines can also be used to suppress or delay oestrus in female dogs.

Above: *Castration of male dogs aids the management of excessively boisterous or inappropriate sexual behavior.*

Neutering males

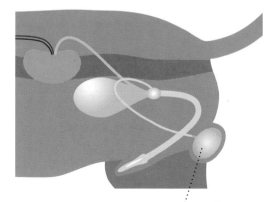

The testicles are removed from the scrotum (or the abdomen if they are not properly descended).

getting the timing right is very important for females. This is because the uterus has a much higher blood supply at the time of a season than it does between seasons, and spaying is much easier and safer when the female dog is between seasons. For this reason, female dogs are usually spayed three months after their first (or subsequent) season, to ensure that the operation is as straightforward as possible.

Post-surgical neutering care

The evening after an anesthetic, dogs are often sleepy and wobbly and may find it hard to regulate their body temperature, so they may chill easily.

Dogs may also feel queasy and be unwilling to eat or may vomit after eating. Offer a small amount of light, easily digestible food, such as chicken and rice, but avoid large meals.

Keep a close eye on wounds and do not allow dogs to lick them. Use an Elizabethan collar or a neck brace to prevent licking if necessary.

Rest dogs with sutures until the wound has healed and the sutures have been removed. Ask your veterinarian to clarify what level of rest your dog will need, or restrict your pet to one or two five-minute walks on his/her leash daily. Do not allow off-leash exercise.

Breeding dogs

Breeding a litter of puppies seems like such an attractive idea, but there are pros and cons to consider. It is not just a matter of needing the space to rear a litter of bouncy puppies, who will cause a great deal of mess and mayhem. It is also important to ensure that you breed only from the most healthy and well-adjusted dogs and that you will be able to find good homes for the puppies. In addition, breeding can be dangerous for the female dog. She could suffer from diseases associated with her pregnancy. She might even be unable to deliver and feed her puppies naturally and may also need a cesarean section. Her puppies may also need hand-rearing. Bear in mind that you will have to protect both mother and puppies against disease and keep them healthy. All in all, breeding is an expensive business at the best of times. Costs can spiral and you may not be able to claim on veterinary fees insurance if things go wrong. On the other hand, breeding a litter can be great fun and extremely rewarding.

Preparing to breed your dog

Before breeding, assess parental conformation and behavior, as it would be unwise to breed a dog with any conformational problems, diseases, or a particularly challenging, difficult, or aggressive personality. Good conformation involves having a healthy body shape that does not predispose a dog to injuries or disease. In addition, it is possible for your veterinarian to carry out a number of tests, depending on the breed of dog involved, to help ascertain that only the healthiest animals are used for breeding and to reduce the chance of genetic diseases being passed on to the next generation. Such tests are extremely important in purebred puppies, giving breeders and purchasers confidence that they are breeding healthy puppies for which they should be able to command an appropriate

What to expect: the first season

Swollen vulva.

Vaginal discharge, bloody for around ten days, then clear.

Attractive to male dogs.

Mating may occur at any stage, but is most likely to occur and result in conception twelve to fifteen days after the bleeding starts.

Mating can involve the female and male dogs locking together and being unable to move apart until twenty to thirty minutes have passed.

Should an unwanted mating occur, seek urgent veterinary advice to discuss the possible options.

price. It may also be wise to test crossbreeds intended for breeding, particularly if matings are planned that combine breeds with similar disease profiles.

Examples of pre-breeding tests include hip and elbow scoring to try to ascertain how likely the prospective parent is to pass on hip dysplasia and elbow dysplasia; hearing testing; and genetic tests for certain eye diseases, as well as eye examinations.

• Hip scoring involves an objective assessment of an X-ray of the dog's hips for signs of hip dysplasia.

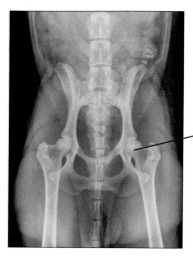
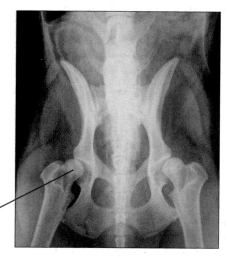

These X-rays show a dog with good conformation (left) and one with hip dysplasia (right).

Here, the ball and socket of the hip joint fit together tightly.

The squarer femur fits poorly into the flatter socket.

A number of criteria are examined, and only dogs with hip scores or assessments better than the breed average should be used for breeding.

• Elbow dysplasia scoring similarly involves assessment of X-rays of the elbows to check that the dog does not have early signs of abnormal elbow development that could be inherited.

• Genetic eye tests check for a number of hereditary eye diseases in a range of breeds. If both parents are clear, the puppies will not inherit the disease. However, parents that are carriers or are affected with these eye diseases would pass them on to their puppies.

• Hearing tests may also be carried out.

• There are genetic tests for various metabolic conditions and for blood-clotting disorders.

Before breeding, it is also important to ensure that parent dogs are a healthy weight and are up-to-date

Below: Pre-breeding tests are vital. Hip, elbow, eye, and genetic tests for myopathy (muscle disorder) are advisable in Labrador Retrievers.

on worming and vaccinations. It may also be advisable to test them for certain sexually transmitted diseases, such as herpes virus and brucellosis. In some countries (but not the U.S.), breeding dogs can be vaccinated against herpes virus to try to prevent infection during pregnancy, which can cause infertility and the death of puppies.

Typically, male and female dogs are subjected to pre-breeding tests once they are mature, but before being mated. They should not be bred until they are physically mature, and the age at which they achieve maturity depends on their breed and type. However, as a general rule it is best to wait until dogs are at least two years old before breeding them.

Practical considerations

The normal female dog is usually most fertile twelve to fifteen days after she starts to bleed, and mating may be carried out every two days while the female dog is receptive to the male during this window. Tests can be done to pinpoint the timing of ovulation and increase the chance of successful mating. This is particularly important for female dogs that do not choose to stand, for whom mating may not be possible, or in cases where assistance may be needed when tests show the female dog to be fertile. There are two alternative methods of testing:

• A veterinarian can take vaginal swabs and examine the cell types present. These indicate the best timing of mating.

• A blood test is taken on day seven after the first sign of bleeding and then every one or two days to check for an intermediate increase in progesterone. This

Female dogs are normally receptive to males when they are at their most fertile.

signals that ovulation will occur soon. Most female dogs are then fertile and can be mated two days later. However, it is a good idea to retest and look for a high level of progesterone to confirm ovulation, as some dogs take more than two days to reach this stage.

Mating

During mating, the male dog generally climbs onto the female dog's back as he penetrates her. His penis normally becomes trapped within the female dog's vaginal muscles (tying), linking the dogs together. The male may climb off at this point, but the dogs can remain tied and stand back-to-back for a few minutes. Attempts to separate the male and female dog are likely to be unsuccessful and may cause injury. Finally, everything relaxes and they are free to move apart.

Pregnancy

In early pregnancy, there are few signs that anything is going on, although female dogs may experience an increase in appetite and show behavioral changes, such as becoming calmer. Blood tests from around twenty-five days of pregnancy can detect changes in hormonal levels, confirming pregnancy. An ultrasound scan can reveal the presence of embryonic vesicles containing developing puppies. Within a matter of days, individual puppies can be seen in more detail and heartbeats can be picked up that confirm their viability. Attempts to count developing puppies are likely to be inaccurate, as it can be difficult to distinguish between different puppies on the ultrasound screen and some deeper-lying puppies may not be detectable.

By four to five weeks of pregnancy, enlargement of the uterus may be palpable and the tummy may be starting to drop and change shape. At this stage it is advisable to gradually change the female dog onto a puppy food and increase the number of meals fed in a day so that she can benefit from the higher levels of the nutrients she needs to grow healthy puppies.

Preparing for the birth

Pregnancy normally lasts for around sixty-three days from conception. Toward the end of her pregnancy, a female dog will become very swollen and cumbersome. She will find it difficult to get comfortable and may find it hard to eat. Her milk glands and teats will become swollen, and it is important to check that they do not become hot and hard, indicating mastitis.

A pregnant female dog will start to exhibit nesting behavior and will try out different dark corners in the

Below: *A well-designed whelping box is a comfortable and safe environment for both the female dog and her puppies.*

house as she prepares herself for whelping (giving birth). At this stage you should provide her with a whelping box or equivalent area, with her bed inside. Depending on the size of the dog, a whelping area ideally includes a bed at one end, made from familiar-smelling blankets and towels that can be washed or discarded when soiled, and a newspaper-lined area for feeding, where the puppies will also relieve themselves. Ideally, the whelping area should have a low barrier around it so that the female dog can get out when she wants to, leaving the puppies enclosed and safe.

Whelping

The sequence of events is as follows:
• The first sign of whelping is generally a drop in the female dog's temperature from about 100°F to 98.6°F (38°C to 37°C) or lower. Most female dogs will start whelping within twenty-four hours of such a temperature drop. It is a good idea, therefore, to monitor a female dog's temperature twice daily from around day sixty of pregnancy.

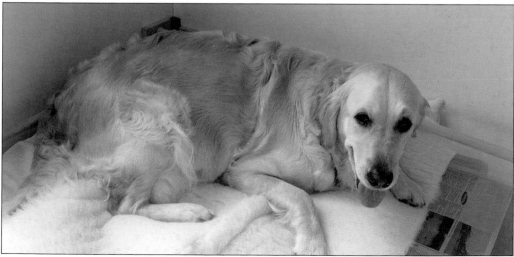

• The temperature drop is followed by signs of restlessness and sometimes trembling or even vomiting, which herald the onset of labor. This stage generally lasts 12–24 hours.

• Once the female dog starts to have visible abdominal contractions and strains, she is ready to start delivering puppies. They generally follow within one to two hours, with one puppy being delivered every one to two hours. Labor is normally completed within twelve to twenty-four hours. Each puppy is normally followed by a placenta; ideally, you should count the placentas and puppies to ensure that no placentas are left inside the female dog. However, the female dog may eat her placentas, so you may not see them all unless you are particularly vigilant.

Caring for the young puppies

Young puppies are born blind, deaf, and helpless. Initially, they rely on their mother for warmth, feeding,

and even the stimulation to pass urine and feces, which they do as she licks them. It is only as they develop that they become seeing, hearing, and mobile; their eyes and ears open at seven to ten days old. At first, they squirm on their tummies but soon rise onto their limbs; as their mobility improves, they start to venture out of the nest and explore their surroundings.

Normal puppies feed regularly and fall asleep soon afterwards. In the beginning, they sleep for two hours or so and then wake to feed again. Healthy puppies are sleek and plump, squeaking only briefly when hungry and sleeping when satiated. Thin-looking, noisy puppies that do not seem to settle may not be getting enough food. They can quickly deteriorate, weaken,

Newborn puppies need a good lick from mom to stimulate breathing.

Left: *Between the delivery of each puppy, the mother rests and often feeds the puppies that are already born. This helps stimulate further uterine contractions.*

and die. Rapidly address any signs of insatiable hunger, as the female dog may need increased feeding or medication to aid her milk production. The puppies may require top-up feeding with a milk replacer.

By three to four weeks of age, the puppies will be eating some of the softened puppy food offered to their mothers, and by about six weeks they will be receiving nearly all the nutrients they need from puppy food. They generally continue to feed from their mothers for about another two weeks.

Preparing puppies for their new home

Even before they leave their mother, puppies can learn something about socializing and toilet training. At four to six weeks old you can allow them a little freedom to accompany their mother outside to relieve themselves, which helps establish early house training. In addition, they can be socialized with other family pets and children, although they should not mix with other puppies or other unvaccinated dogs, as this can be a risk factor for infectious disease.

Puppies should be wormed regularly from two to four weeks of age. They may also need flea and other antiparasite treatments and can be vaccinated from six to eight weeks of age. They can leave for their new home at around eight weeks old. Prepare an information sheet explaining what treatments they have been given, what puppy food they are fed, and how many meals they eat daily. Provide a sample of their own food for the new owners to mix in with a new supply. Leaving with a bit of their own unwashed bedding from the whelping area will help puppies feel secure and at home in their new family.

How to take a dog's temperature

If the dog is average-sized, use a rectal thermometer dipped in a little lubricating jelly and insert it around 1 in (2 cm) into the dog's rectum (less for smaller dogs). Hold it with the tip directed across to the side slightly for a minimum of thirty seconds. Wipe clean with dry tissue and read the temperature quickly. The normal temperature of the dog is around 100°F (38°C).

A digital thermometer is ideal to use.

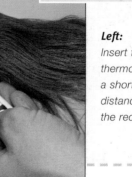

Left: *Insert the thermometer a short distance into the rectum.*

Part 2

Guide to health problems

Most dogs are healthy most of the time and it is important not to let a discussion of what can go wrong become too frightening. Having access to information about health problems can help you understand the disease processes that may occur. However well you look after your dogs and aim to provide them with just the right balance of food, exercise, love, attention, and preventative treatments, there will still be times when they suffer from disease.

Recognizing the first signs of problems at an early stage enables you to organize the most appropriate treatment promptly and helps dogs recover from disease as quickly as possible. Both medical and surgical treatments can be expensive, and costs can spiral in complicated cases. Insurance for veterinarian's fees is recommended, as it offers you the potential to file a claim for excessive costs. It can give you the peace of mind to choose the most appropriate investigations and treatments for your animal without having to make decisions based on economics alone.

A basic knowledge of your dog's anatomy is vital and can help alert you when health problems arise.

Below: *Thorough examination and, where necessary, further investigation, allows an accurate diagnosis to be made, enabling effective treatment.*

A veterinary examination

The information you can give the veterinarian is very helpful when looked at together with a thorough examination of the dog. During an examination your veterinarian can check your dog's vital signs (temperature, pulse, and respiration), as well as look at him and examine his entire body. A thorough examination can determine whether or not a dog is suffering from heart or breathing problems, how his circulation is functioning, and whether or not he is dehydrated. It can help reveal any lumps or bumps in the skin or underlying tissues, or within the abdominal cavity. Manipulating the neck, back, and limbs can help identify orthopedic problems, and examining the eyes, ears, and face, as well as the dog's response to certain stimuli, can allow the nervous system to be assessed.

Often, a diagnosis can follow a thorough clinical examination. However, further investigation is frequently needed to confirm a diagnosis or assess the degree of any problem that has been identified. Typical diagnostic tests include blood tests, X-rays, and ultrasound scanning, along with a range of other tests.

Blood tests may reveal problems with the red or white blood cells or platelets, or with biochemistry markers that give indications regarding liver and kidney function as well as bowel, heart, and bone problems. Blood tests can also allow **diabetes mellitus** and other hormonal problems to be identified.

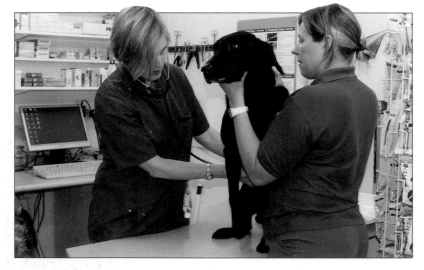

Left: *A thorough clinical examination, facilitated by appropriate restraint of the affected dog, can yield a great deal of information.*

Above: *Ear examination using an otoscope is easiest with the dog's head held steady.*

Other diagnostic procedures include X-ray, which examines bones and other tissues, and ultrasound scanning and MRI, both of which image soft tissue structures in the body.

Once a clear diagnosis has been made, it is possible to assess the best course of treatment. This may involve surgical correction of certain problems or may be based on medication, such as antibiotics to fight bacterial infections, anti-inflammatory medicines and analgesics to relieve pain, as well as medicines that aid heart function, treat hormone disorders, and help control other diseases. Surgical treatments, usually necessitating general anesthesia, may be used to remove masses, stabilize fractures, and treat other orthopedic conditions, as well as to remove abnormal structures. Other treatments include chemotherapy and radiotherapy for cancers, and complementary treatments such as acupuncture to aid pain control. Nutraceuticals (food supplements that aid management of disease) can be helpful in some cases, and physiotherapy and hydrotherapy are also beneficial for many dogs.

A veterinary examination can include assessing:
• The eyes (using an ophthalmoscope)
• The ears (using an otoscope)
• The teeth and jaws
• The gums (relating to circulation)
• The skin
• The sounds of the heart and lungs (using a stethoscope)
• The abdomen (by palpation, or detailed feeling)
• The genitals and anus
• The limbs and back

? *What are*
X-rays

X-rays involve making an image of the shadow of a body part when exposed to an X-ray beam. Although this is most useful for looking at bone, X-rays can also allow assessment of the size, shape, and position of internal organs.

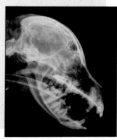

Skin diseases

Skin disease in dogs is not uncommon and can take a number of forms. Problems may be widespread all over the body, but the paws and ears are particularly prone to problems.

Symptoms

Symptoms of skin disease include:
- Loss of hair, the development of spots, a rash or skin discoloration, and itchiness.
- Affected skin may appear discolored, thickened, and more flaky or greasy than normal.
- Even if they are not itchy, affected dogs may have suppurating or oozing skin lesions.

Diagnosis

Diagnosis may necessitate carrying out tests to differentiate between some common problems that may have similar symptoms.
- Swabs taken from infected areas can be sent to a laboratory to identify the bacteria present and the antibiotics to which they are sensitive.
- In the case of wounds, the cause of disease may be clear, but other conditions may require further investigation. For example, some types of ringworm fluoresce apple-green under ultraviolet light. They can be identified by shining a Wood's lamp (which emits ultraviolet light) onto the skin lesion. Ringworm can also be detected by microscopic examination of affected skin debris and hairs, and by culture

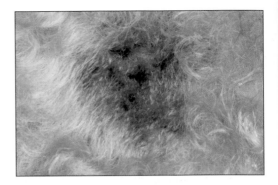

Above: *Reddening and thickening of the skin, and hair loss, are common signs of skin disease.*

of debris on a special culture plate containing a color-change indicator that changes color after a few days if ringworm is present.
- Hair combing, skin scrapes, and hair plucks may be needed to identify any parasites present, such as lice, mites, ticks, or fleas. Skin and hair samples may need to be examined under a microscope for mites and lice.
- An effective broad-spectrum antiparasitic treatment may be used to exclude parasite problems that can otherwise cause itchiness and secondary skin infections.
- Tests include a food allergy trial (see page 58). Blood or skin allergy tests look for antibodies in the blood or a reaction in the skin against certain pollens, dust mites, and other species to identify environmental allergies.
- Skin biopsies (surgical sampling of an area of skin and examination of it under a microscope) can also yield useful information.

- Blood tests may allow identification of skin diseases that relate to underlying diseases associated with other body systems, such as **hormone problems**.

Treatments

Treatments depend on the cause of the problem.
- Antiparasitic medicines and antibiotics or antifungal medicines treat parasites, bacterial infections, or ringworm.
- Avoiding allergens can be helpful, and special diets can be used for food-allergic dogs.
- Antihistamines help reduce allergic reactions, and steroids may also be used to reduce allergies, inflammation, and itchiness.
- Hyposensitization treatment can build up a dog's tolerance of things he is allergic to by injecting increasing tiny doses of the offending agent or allergen.
- Skin lumps may need to be removed, while other underlying problems obviously need

? *What is a*
Skin scrape

A skin scrape is carried out by rubbing an abnormal area of skin with a sharp blade and then wiping any debris onto a microscope slide and examining it under the microscope. Plucked hairs and fluid squeezed from abraded skin can also be examined. This allows mites and other parasites to be identified, as well as skin bacteria and yeast infections, including ringworm.

specific treatments.
- Essential fatty acid supplements can increase the general health of the skin and can be helpful in virtually all types of skin disease. A variety of other supplements help promote healthy skin.

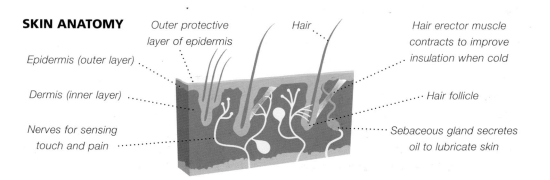

SKIN ANATOMY

Outer protective layer of epidermis

Hair

Hair erector muscle contracts to improve insulation when cold

Epidermis (outer layer)

Dermis (inner layer)

Nerves for sensing touch and pain

Hair follicle

Sebaceous gland secretes oil to lubricate skin

Pyoderma

Bacterial infections of the skin are extremely common; while a problem may exist in its own right, pyoderma (skin infection) is often a consequence of another disease that has affected the health of the dog's skin and made it more prone to infection. Bacteria and yeast organisms are present on the surface of the skin at all times and rarely cause problems. However, if they penetrate the top layer of skin, invade hair follicles, and cause infection of the structure of the skin, they can cause pustules, rashes, and areas of reddened, moist, bald oozing skin (sometimes known as wet eczema) to develop.

DEEP PYODERMA

Infection can travel all the way through the skin and result in abscesses and infected tracts that may drain through the skin and be extremely painful.

Symptoms

- Itchiness is a common consequence of pyoderma; affected dogs often spread infection, seeding it into new areas of skin by scratching and nibbling. This in itself causes further damage and allows more extensive infection.
- Often, by the time the dog is seen by a veterinarian, the signs of infection are so severe that they have obscured any original symptoms caused by the underlying problem.

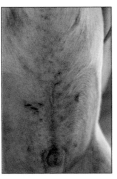

Above: Pyoderma may cause a raised, itchy skin rash, which can easily spread.

This means that it is very common for a dog with skin disease to need treatment for its pyoderma as well as its underlying problems, which themselves need addressing if recurrent bouts of pyoderma are to be avoided.

Diagnosis Swabs may allow the type of bacteria present to be identified (often one of a range of *Staphylococci*) and also identify yeast infections, such as *Malassezia* and *Candida*, which can cause very similar skin disease.

Treatment Long courses of treatment are often needed to treat pyoderma. Courses of antibiotics may need to be given for six to twelve weeks or sometimes longer to treat bacterial infections. Yeast infections are often treated with medicated washes or shampoos, and these may also need to be repeated for weeks or months.

PODODERMATITIS

This deep infection of the tissues of the feet is very painful and can cause lameness and severe sensitivity of the feet. It can also cause nail bed infections (paronychia) that can lead to loss of nails.

Symptoms

- Itchiness and the development of sores between the toes and pads and on the skin around them.

Treatment In addition to antibiotic treatment and therapy for any underlying problems, such as

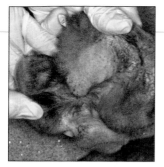

Left: Chronic thickening of the skin on the paws is often associated with pododermatitis.

allergies or parasites, foot washes in a mild antiseptic may be necessary.

FURUNCULOSIS

This is a deep infection of the skin, most commonly seen in warm, moist parts of the body. The feet can be affected, as can the nasal area. However, the most common form is anal furunculosis, seen in the anal region in dogs with low tail carriage.

Symptoms

• Abscessation and tracts of infection.

Treatment Medicines to reduce inflammation. Some cases may need surgical treatment.

SKIN FOLD PYODERMA

This condition most commonly affects breeds with saggy skin and squashed-up faces. It can be seen in the facial folds in brachycephalic breeds, such as Bulldogs and Pugs, and also in the lip folds and the genital area.

Symptoms

• Skin folds may be reddened and itchy, and a discharge from affected skin may be evident.

Treatment Antibiotic medicines and creams, plus thorough cleaning and drying of affected areas. Surgical removal of skin folds may be helpful in extreme cases. Petroleum jelly may also be used as a barrier to help prevent reinfection.

ACNE/IMPETIGO

This is a common problem in the facial area of young and growing puppies. It may spontaneously resolve but can need antibiotic treatment.

ELBOW CALLUSES

These are often seen in older dogs, particularly those that do not sleep on a thick, soft bed.

Symptoms

• Skin over pressure points, such as the elbows (but also possibly the hips and parts of the paws and hocks), often becomes hairless and thickened.

• Skin may sometimes become infected or ulcerated.

Treatment In the latter cases, long courses of medication may be required. Surgical treatment may be necessary. Petroleum jelly may help keep thickened skin healthy and supple, and affected dogs may need thicker beds.

Left: Reddened pustules on this young Boxer's lips are typical signs of acne.

Parasitic skin diseases

Parasitic skin diseases are common and should always be considered as a possible cause of skin disease.

Symptoms
- Hair loss, itchiness, and skin damage.
- Some parasites may also cause problems such as **anemia**.

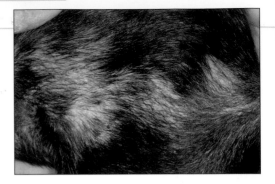

Above: The presence of an itchy rash and hair loss are often associated with parasitic skin disease.

FLEAS

These are the most common skin parasites. They range from about 1–3 mm in length, depending on type. Different species exist that primarily infect rodents, birds, cats, dogs, and even humans, but all can affect dogs.

Symptoms
- Fleas are visible to the naked eye and can often be seen crawling and jumping between the hair shafts when the dog's hair is parted. Adult fleas lay hundreds of eggs, which fall from the animal and can develop in carpets and gaps between flooring, providing a constant source of reinfection.

Treatment with veterinary spot-on products on a monthly basis is the most effective way to kill adult fleas, but other products may be needed to treat the home and the animal's bedding to prevent flea egg development.

Fleas can carry tapeworms. Make sure affected dogs are up to date on their worming.

TICKS

Ticks live predominantly in damp, forested areas and may also be found on farmland, as they can affect deer and sheep. Ticks crawl onto passing dogs, embed their mouthparts, and suck blood.

Symptoms
- Ticks cause little skin irritation but can introduce skin infection, causing a red, swollen area. They can also transmit infections into the blood, including **Lyme disease**.

Treatment Although anti-tick products can be used on the skin in tick-prone areas, it is also important to groom dogs after forest and grassland walks. Try to remove any ticks before they embed or as soon after as possible.

LICE

Lice, measuring 1–2 mm long, can sometimes be found in a dog's coat, causing irritation and potentially anemia (some types suck blood). "Nits," or lice eggs, may be found on the hair.

Symptoms
- Intense itchiness and irritation.

Treatment Easy with antiparasitic products.

REMOVING TICKS

Do not try to burn off a tick with a cigarette, or use petroleum jelly or nail varnish. Although the latter methods work, they take too long.

1. *Swab the tick with alcohol, then remove it with tweezers.*

2. *Once the tick is secure, twist the hook to pull the tick free.*

3. *Check that the mouth-parts are not left in the skin; they can cause infection.*

Above: *An embedded tick near this dog's eye could cause infection if not promptly removed.*

MANGE MITES

Mange mites cannot be seen with the naked eye but live on and in the skin of affected dogs.

Symptoms
• Itchiness and thickening of the skin.

Diagnosis A skin scrape or skin biopsy may be necessary. Several different types can be seen.

Treatment Although sarcoptic mange and cheyletiella mites can be easy to treat, demodectic mange tends to occur in dogs that are particularly susceptible and can be hard to resolve completely. Regular spot-on treatments or insecticidal baths may be needed.

LEISHMANIASIS

This is caused by a tiny parasite *(Leishmania)* that can be transmitted to dogs by sand fly and, possibly, midge bites in certain parts of the world (but rarely in the U.S.). The parasites infect immune cells and cause a range of problems.

• Skin thickening and crustiness (but not normally itchiness).

• Weight loss and immune disease. Leishmaniasis can be fatal and is transmissible to humans.

Avoiding leishmaniasis involves avoiding endemic areas and using fly-repelling skin products and collars to try to prevent transmission.

Left: *Mange can cause areas of thinning of the hair that cause a "moth-eaten" appearance.*

EAR MITES

These are another common parasitic problem. *Otodectes* mites can infest the ear canals.

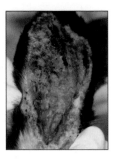

Above: *Severe crusting of the ear flap due to disease.*

Symptoms

- Intense irritation, itchiness of the ears, and an increase in ear wax production.
- A dark brown, smelly discharge exuding from the ears.
- Affected dogs may also develop secondary bacterial and yeast infections, causing a discharge of pus.

Diagnosis The mites are hard to see with the naked eye, but can be easily seen using a 10x magnifying lens on an otoscope, or may be detected on an ear swab.

Treatment usually involves ear drops containing antiparasitic medicines. These generally need to be used for two weeks to ensure that the mite infection has been completely resolved.

Ear infections

Bacteria and yeast infections can cause ear infections on their own.

Symptoms

- Ear discharge containing pus, reddening of the ear lining, and ear pain.
- Infections that extend beyond the outer ear canal into the middle or inner ear may also cause the dog to become unwell, develop a fever, and possibly experience loss of balance and a head tilt. Rupture of the eardrum may follow and hearing may be temporarily or permanently affected.

Diagnosis Laboratory examination of an ear swab can identify the cause of infection and help determine the most appropriate medication.

Treatment Medicated ear drops are often used, as long as the eardrum is intact. If ruptured, using ear drops can cause loss of balance and should therefore be avoided. Systemic medicines must be used instead.

Ear infections are particularly common in dogs with narrow ear canals or very hairy ears, such

> **!** *Did you know*
> ## *Aural hematoma*
>
> *Anything that causes ear irritation and head shaking can result in an aural hematoma. This occurs when a blood vessel between the two layers of skin that form the ear flap bursts and causes a large blood blister to form in the ear flap, making it swell up. It can be possible to drain aural hematomas, or surgical treatment may be necessary. In either case, some scarring inevitably results and the affected dog may be left with a slight "cauliflower ear."*

as Poodles, as ears of this type may be unable to self-cleanse naturally. Dogs with underlying allergic skin disease may also be predisposed to ear infections.

In some cases, regular (e.g., twice-weekly) ear cleaning with an inert ear cleanser can be helpful. In others, surgery may be needed to open up the ear canal. Hair plucking may be advisable.

Foreign bodies

A head tilt and ear pain can also be the first sign that a foreign body is lodged within the ear. Grass seed heads are a common problem and can get into the ear canal after a dog has run through long grass. Removal with forceps using an otoscope may be possible in a conscious dog,

How to
Clean the ears

Apply cleanser deep into the vertical ear canal. Massage well to disperse the drops. Wipe away debris that floats up to the ear orifice with clean cotton balls and repeat the process until the ear is clean. Dogs with hairy ears may first need hair plucking. This can be done by groomers; it can also be done a little at a time at home by owners. Be careful, though; it can hurt.

but sometimes a general anesthetic is needed to enable the dog to stay still enough for this procedure.

ALLERGIES AFFECTING THE EARS

Allergies to food or items in the environment such as pollens and dusts can cause allergic skin disease **(atopy)**. Often, one of the first signs that there may be a problem involves the ears becoming inflamed and more susceptible to disease. This can be particularly marked with allergies to bedding, when the hairless part of the ear is in contact with the allergen and can be significantly affected.

EAR ANATOMY

The ear canal goes almost straight down before turning in toward the drum.

Medicines prescribed need to be given deep into the external vertical part of the ear canal. The area can then be massaged to help disperse drops toward the eardrum.

The eardrum transmits sounds to the inner ear.

Allergic skin disease

Unlike humans, dogs primarily express their allergies through their skin. Some allergies can cause reddened and watery eyes and even, perhaps, a slight nasal discharge. However, most cause itchiness of the skin, resulting in scratching, nibbling, and licking at the skin and hair, which leads to self-damage and saliva staining that turns pale fur brown.

CONTACT ALLERGIES

Skin contact with certain substances may result in allergic disease.

Symptoms

- Affected dogs may develop a well-defined area that has been directly affected (for instance, by a chemical or medicine to which the dog is allergic).
- Allergies to flea saliva may also cause localized reaction around a flea bite.
- Allergies can occur to pollens and dusts, causing a more widespread reaction.

INHALED ALLERGIES

Many allergens are inhaled or taken in through the mouth, but they cause a reaction in the skin. Tree, weed, and grass pollens can act in this way, as can dust and molds. (See also page 140.)

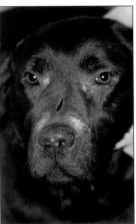

Above: Facial hair loss can be a consequence of parasitic, allergic, or immune-mediated disease.

FOOD ALLERGIES

Food allergies are also common. Dogs can develop allergies to any constituents of their food, and this can also cause them to develop itchy skin. Identification of the problem is usually best achieved by feeding a hypoallergenic food (ideally one based on a single carbohydrate and protein source or hydrolyzed ingredients that the animal is unlikely to be allergic to) for a period of four to six weeks. During this time no other treats – in fact nothing other than water and the prescription food – should pass the dog's lips. If this resolves the skin problem, then the hypoallergenic diet may be continued, or normal food types may be gradually added back into the diet until the problem is identified.

ATOPY

Atopy, or allergic skin disease, is a common problem.

Diagnosis Identifying the types of allergens involved may be achieved by changing the dog's environment and seeing if his skin improves. Blood allergy testing and patch testing of the skin can also allow identification of common allergens. Groups of grass, tree, and weed pollens can be tested, alongside house dust and storage mites, molds, fleas, skin dander from other species (e.g., cat), and a range of other allergens.

Treatment Once the problem has been identified, the veterinarian can offer advice about the dog's management (for example, how to reduce dust levels in the home for a dog with a dust mite allergy).

Hyposensitization treatments can be prepared for the affected dog (see page 51). In addition, affected dogs may be treated with antihistamines to reduce their allergic response and essential fatty acid supplements to try to increase the health of the skin and make it less reactive. Steroid treatments are also used in some cases to try to reduce inflammation and itchiness. Other medicines may be used that affect the skin's allergic and immune responses to make them less itchy.

Immune-mediated disease

Some skin diseases are immune-mediated in origin. This means that the diseases result from the body's immune system attacking its own skin cells and causing damage. These diseases can occur all over the dog's body, but commonly affected areas include the paws, nail beds, and junctions between different types of tissues, such as at the mouth, eyelids, and nose.

Symptoms

- Itchy and painful ulcerated areas may develop, as well as a crusty thickening of the skin, leading to excessive dandruff formation.

Diagnosis can be made after laboratory examination of biopsy samples taken from affected tissues.

What are
Allergy tests

Environmental allergies, such as those involving pollens, dusts, and fungal spores, may be detectable with blood or skin allergy testing. Blood allergy testing involves running a panel of tests for antibodies to common problem items. Skin allergy testing involves injecting a tiny quantity of common-problem items into the skin in a spaced-out grid and waiting to see if a substantial skin swelling results, indicating an allergy. Once relevant allergens have been identified for a particular dog, they may be avoided or hyposensitization treatment may be initiated.

Treatment involves using essential fatty acid supplements to improve the general health of the skin. Steroid treatments and medicines that have an effect on the immune system are also commonly used.

Below: Areas of skin infection can result from allergic skin disease. Tests can identify the cause.

Wounds

Skin wounds commonly follow injuries and dog fights. Some small wounds may heal well without treatment, but it is advisable to get all wounds checked out promptly by a veterinarian. Depending on the site of the wound, the veterinarian will be able to assess whether or not deeper structures, such as nerves, muscles, and blood vessels, are damaged and whether the chest or abdominal cavity is involved (see also pages 142 and 190).

TREATING WOUNDS

Small wounds may need nothing more than cleaning to allow them to heal. However, extensive, full thickness skin wounds that expose underlying tissues may require surgery so that any deeper structures can be repaired and the wound closed. Some puncture wounds are best left at least partially open to allow drainage of infected material and debris. Wounds that involve areas of skin loss may need more than one surgical treatment, or skin grafting techniques, and some need to heal as open wounds. Most wounds are contaminated or infected and require antibiotic treatment, and affected dogs may also need pain relief.

HOW DO WOUNDS HEAL?

A clean wound brought together surgically with appropriate stitching can heal by what is called "primary intention." This means that the two edges of skin bond rapidly, and although the scar takes time to reach full strength, the skin

HOW WOUNDS HEAL

Wounds that are not sutured heal by "secondary intention," a process that involves the following stages.

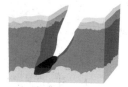  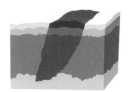 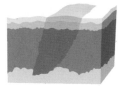

1. Blood clot and other products of tissue damage accumulate within the wound, and the edges contract, reducing its size.

2. A bed of reddish, textured granulation tissue forms in the base of the wound and stabilizes it. A scab forms at its surface.

3. New skin grows from the granulating edge at up to 1–2 mm per day and gradually extends across the wound, but under the scab, to seal it.

4. Gradually, the scar tissue is replaced by normal tissue and the skin becomes supple again. Massage and physiotherapy may help.

Left: Wounds that are infected and involve damaged skin may not benefit from surgical repair.

retains its mobility and suppleness and has a good degree of strength by the time the stitches are removed after ten to fourteen days.

Infected wounds or wounds involving areas of skin loss or those in high-motion areas, such as over a joint, may not be able to heal by primary intention. Instead, the wound may need to be left open, cleaned regularly (bathed twice daily with dilute antiseptic or a weak salt solution), and allowed to heal by "secondary intention." This involves a number of stages.

What is
MRSA

Methicillin-resistant Staphylococcus aureus (MRSA) *can occur in dogs and cause problems with wound healing. This bacterium can also act as a source of infection for owners. It can be identified on laboratory examination of a swab from the affected animal.*

BURNS

Thermal burns, such as scalds and frostbite, can be considered as a type of wound. Skin damage due to intense heat (e.g., being too close to a fire or even lying up against a radiator) or extreme cold (e.g., being out in subfreezing temperatures) causes failure of the blood supply to an area of skin, which then dies away. Treatment may involve surgical removal of the affected area and primary intention healing as healthy tissue is brought into alignment over the affected area. More often, burns may need to be managed as open wounds. In severe cases, fluid loss from burns may be so extreme that the animal requires intravenous fluids by drip to replace fluid oozing from damaged areas.

HOW BURNS HEAL

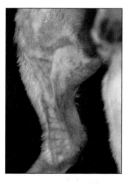

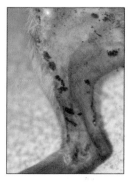

Before: Burns may involve a large area of skin loss. Infection and fluid loss are common.

After: A combination of antibiotics and topical treatment can result in rapid healing.

Skin tumors

Skin tumors are one of the most common types of tumor seen in dogs. Although a high proportion of skin tumors are benign, some types of malignant tumors can either invade tissue around themselves or spread through the body and damage other organs. Therefore, it is important to recognize skin tumors promptly and to treat them appropriately.

Above: *Masses next to vital structures need prompt investigation.*

Right: *Masses showing color changes also require immediate attention.*

Symptoms

- Initially, masses generally appear in the skin as a small bump, which may grow over a period of time. Some barely change at all from the point they are first seen, while others grow rapidly and change appearance.
- Hair loss may occur over the mass; it may exhibit a color change from the surrounding skin, and it may also ulcerate and weep or bleed.
- The position of a tumor may affect nearby parts of the body. For example, eyelid tumors can cause eye damage and may need to be removed promptly. Even fatty lumps can cause problems if they interfere with limb movement.

Diagnosis At an initial appointment, the veterinarian can assess the mass in terms of its position, depth within the skin, whether it is attached to underlying tissues, and whether it has the appearance of any particular type of tumor. It may be possible to measure the mass with calipers and then monitor its growth over a period of time. Further investigation may be recommended. A fine needle aspiration biopsy involves passing a needle into the mass and then using it to suck out some cells, which can be examined under a microscope. This may confirm

> **?** *What is a* **Biopsy**
>
> *Using local or general anesthesia, a sample of diseased tissue is surgically removed and submitted to a laboratory for examination under a microscope. Evaluation of the cell types and structures present can allow diagnosis of different types of cancer, auto-immune, and inflammatory diseases.*

the presence of fat cells, indicating a fatty lump that is likely to be benign (lipoma). Alternatively, it can confirm the presence of other types of cells, such as mast cells found in a mast cell tumor. A surgical biopsy (removing part or all of the mass) may be taken under general anesthesia. Again, examining the tissue under a microscope allows the cell types present to be identified. Blood tests and other diagnostic tests may be needed to aid identification of the tumor type and to assess the health of other organs in the body.

Treatment Surgical removal is the most common treatment. Masses are generally easiest to remove while they are still fairly small, and they are less likely to have spread if they are removed promptly after they appear. Depending on the tumor type and its position, the mass may be easy to remove completely. However, if it is difficult or impossible to remove the mass with a rim of normal tissue around it, the mass may then recur.

Depending on the type and position of a mass, radiotherapy and chemotherapy may also be appropriate in some dogs.

Outcome Many individual masses can be removed entirely at a single operation and may never cause a problem again. However, malignant tumor types can cause secondary disease, which can be difficult or even impossible to treat and may in time necessitate euthanasia.

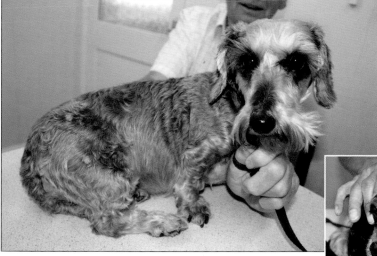

Below: *The head is a common site for warts to develop. This Cavalier King Charles Spaniel is being assessed by a veterinarian.*

Above: *To ensure speedy treatment, all masses should be checked out by a veterinarian to ensure they are not malignant.*

Digestive diseases

Symptoms of digestive diseases generally relate to problems with eating, digesting food, or passing motions.

Symptoms

- Lack of appetite; problems swallowing.
- Vomiting or attempting to vomit.
- Abdominal swelling, weight loss, flatulence.
- Diarrhea and constipation.
- Weakness, a poor coat, and general unhealthiness relating to inadequate assimilation of nutrients in the body.

Diagnosis

Blood tests are commonly used to identify:
- Changes in enzyme levels that can indicate disease in the bowels.
- Deficiencies in digestive enzymes.
- Disorders in the levels of naturally occurring bowel bacteria and changes in levels of protein that relate to bowel function.
- Some infectious bowel diseases.
- The presence of parasites.
- Some types of cancer.

Feces can be analyzed for the presence of:
- Various bacteria and viruses, as well as for signs of inadequate digestion.
- A number of types of parasites.
- Blood in feces, which may indicate bowel wall disease or inflammation.

In some cases further tests may be needed:
- X-rays, ultrasound scanning, and endoscopy to assess diseased or thickened bowel and stomach walls and to identify any lumps or diseased areas.
- Surgically removed biopsy samples from affected tissues or organs can be examined under a microscope in a laboratory. This makes it possible to identify the cell type present and thus the disease involved.

Treatments

- Antibiotics to treat infection.
- Anti-parasitic medicines to treat worms and other parasitic diseases.
- Specific enzyme supplements to aid digestion.
- Anti-inflammatory medicines to reduce inflammation in cases where this is present.
- Medicines to slow bowel transit time and reduce diarrhea, as well as to absorb any toxins from within the bowel.
- Anti-emetics to stop vomiting.
- Oral / intravenous fluids to maintain hydration.

With prompt treatment, many straightforward cases of bowel disease respond well, with no ill effects. However, some chronic problems, as well as severe parasite disease, serious bacterial or viral infections, and some types of inflammatory disease and cancer, can cause ongoing symptoms that are difficult to manage.

THE DIGESTIVE SYSTEM

1. In the mouth, food mixes with saliva, which contains digestive enzymes, and is chewed up to break down the size of the particles.

2. Smaller pieces of food are moved to the back of the tongue where they form into a bolus and are swallowed, traveling in the esophagus, through the chest cavity, and into the stomach in the abdomen.

3. In the stomach, food mixes with acidic digestive juices containing protein-digesting enzymes and is broken down into smaller particles.

4. The particles then pass into the duodenum. Here, enzymes from the pancreas and bile from the liver break down fat to continue the process of reducing food to its constituent fats, proteins, and sugars.

6. In the large intestine, more water is reabsorbed from the bowel contents into the surrounding blood supply, so that fluid levels are conserved and firm feces are formed.

5. In the small intestine these particles, along with minerals, vitamins, and some of the water in the bowel, are absorbed across the gut wall into the intestinal blood system. This passes them to the liver, where they are broken down further.

7. Feces are held in the rectum until passed, when the anal sphincter is opened at a suitable time.

Mouth problems

A number of diseases can cause dogs to experience difficulty in eating.

CRANIOMANDIBULAR OSTEOPATHY

This developmental disease can occur in growing puppies of small terrier breed dogs, generally Cairn Terriers or Westies.

Symptoms

- Jaw stiffness and intense pain.
- Affected dogs often become unwilling to eat, and it may be physically impossible for them to open their mouths wide for examination.

Diagnosis X-rays can reveal abnormal bone deposits around the jaw joints.

Treatment Anti-inflammatory pain-relieving medicines generally control the condition during development until, in most cases, it naturally resolves as the animal matures.

DENTAL DISEASE

This develops when bacteria in the mouth react with food and saliva to cause a deposit of tartar on dogs' teeth. Although minimized by regular brushing and dental chews (see page 18), tartar

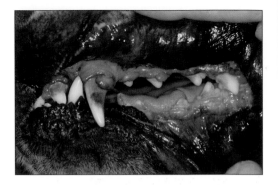

Above: *There is a mass next to this dog's canine tooth. Prompt assessment is advisable, as such tumors can be malignant.*

development on the teeth can lead to infection of adjacent gums (gingivitis). This can lead to tooth root infections, which can undermine and loosen teeth and cause tooth root abscesses.

Symptoms

- Gum or facial swelling and oozing of purulent discharge from the swelling itself or the edge of the tooth. Abscesses are extremely painful and may result in a dog being unwilling to eat.
- Excessive inflammation is also a predisposing factor for the development of mouth epulis (a benign tumor), which can in turn lead to disease in nearby teeth.

Diagnosis X-rays to assess the extent of any damage.

Treatment Diseased teeth may need filling, although teeth with loose roots are generally extracted (removed surgically). Preventing dental disease is better than a cure.

Left: *Mouth pain in terrier puppies can be caused by craniomandibular osteopathy.*

ORAL TUMORS

These are not uncommon in dogs.

Symptoms

- Lumps may develop in the gums, jaw, lip folds, tongue, or even nasal area.
- The lumps cause mouth pain, difficulty eating, and damage to nearby teeth.

Diagnosis X-rays may be needed to aid diagnosis.

Treatment Epulis are benign. They can be reduced in size or removed to prevent damage to nearby teeth. Many other mouth tumors are malignant, can rapidly spread, and damage large areas of the mouth. Early biopsy/removal is paramount. Radiotherapy may benefit some dogs after surgical removal of a tumor.

SALIVARY MUCOCELE

This large swelling forms under the tongue or in the neck due to a blockage in the salivary system.

Symptoms

- Difficulty eating, an increase in salivation, and mouth pain.
- Affected dogs may have a swelling that looks like a mass, although it is generally smoother and more normal in surface appearance than a mouth tumor, which tends to be more irregular in appearance.

Diagnosis Any mouth masses need prompt assessment.

Treatment Anti-inflammatory and antibiotic medication. Surgical draining of the structure or removing the affected salivary gland may be necessary.

FOREIGN BODIES IN THE MOUTH

Symptoms

- Swelling, salivary discharge.
- Mouth pain and difficulty eating.

Diagnosis Fragments of bone can penetrate the gum line; bones or sticks may become lodged across the roof of the mouth between the teeth. Foreign bodies and sticks can penetrate the back of the throat and the esophagus, damaging important nerves and blood vessels to the extent that stick injuries can be fatal.

CLEANING TEETH

Brushing your dog's teeth is vital for good dental care. Veterinarians can tackle more serious problems.

Before: *Tartar on the teeth can lead to infection into the gums and tooth roots.*

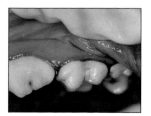

After: *Following a dental descale the teeth have a shiny white appearance.*

Throat problems

Throat conditions can cause various problems.

ESOPHAGEAL DAMAGE

This may result if dogs swallow sharp bones, toys, or other foreign bodies. In addition, narrowing of the esophagus due to scarring can follow injuries, making it difficult for dogs to swallow.

NEUROLOGICAL CONDITIONS

Conditions involving the nerves of the head and throat or the brain may also cause difficulty swallowing.

MEGAESOPHAGUS

This involves distension of the esophagus as it passes through the chest cavity in the space between the lungs. The enlarged esophagus cannot adequately move swallowed food along.

> **!** *Be aware*
> ## *Toys, not sticks*
>
> *It is inadvisable to throw sticks for dogs, as they can cause fatal throat injuries when caught. Always play with appropriate toys instead.*

Food tends to sit in the part of the esophagus located within the chest and is then regurgitated instead of being moved down into the stomach.

Symptoms

- Because swallowing is impaired, dogs tend to be underweight, drool, and regurgitate.
- Dogs may suffer bouts of aspiration pneumonia – a chest infection caused by inhaling food particles.

Left: Dog toys, canine dummies, and balls are appropriate toys for retrieving and play.

MEGAESOPHAGUS

During swallowing, waves of contractions pass food down the normal esophagus to the stomach. Megaesophagus involves distension of the esophagus in the chest in which food may pool.

Food collects in this distended region of the esophagus.

A bolus of food is propelled by esophageal contraction.

? What is Endoscopy

Endoscopy involves sliding a narrow (generally less than 1 cm-diameter) fiber-optic tube housing a video camera into the stomach or lower bowel (or even the lungs, bladder, or uterus) to see the lining and internal structure of these areas.

Diagnosis may be made when X-rays are taken of the chest after eating. Endoscopy can also be helpful.

Treatment In addition to treatment for their underlying condition, affected dogs may be given medicines to aid esophageal muscle contractility. They may also benefit from being fed soft foods from a high feeding bowl and by sitting after feeding to aid gravitational descent of food into the stomach.

Megaesophagus can also occur not only on its own, but also as a consequence of some other disorders. These include **myasthenia gravis** (a disorder that causes muscle weakness), **Addison's disease**, and **hypothyroidism**. It also occurs as a result of the muscle weakness caused by botulism infection and lead poisoning. Megaesophagus can also occur after esophageal injuries and is associated with some congenital diseases (those that develop in the womb) that result in abnormal development or abnormal position of the heart and the main blood vessels in the chest.

Stomach problems

A number of conditions can affect the stomach, and some require urgent veterinary treatment.

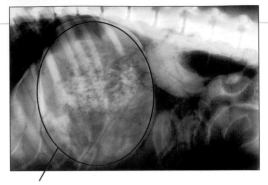

GDV has resulted in the distended stomach outlined in this X-ray. This is a serious condition.

GASTRIC DILATION AND VOLVULUS (GDV)

This is one of the most concerning conditions. Affected dogs can deteriorate rapidly as the expanding stomach (gastric dilation) puts pressure on the heart and lungs and can impede blood circulation. As the stomach swells it can start to rotate (volvulus), cutting off its own blood supply, taking the spleen with it into an abnormal position and potentially damaging the spleen's blood supply, too.

Affected dogs develop signs rapidly after eating and can deteriorate so fast that they can die within hours if not treated promptly. Symptoms of GDV always constitute an emergency situation and necessitate urgent veterinary attention.

Symptoms

- Attempting to vomit without success (see page 196 emergency scenarios).
- Drooling, depression, and weakness.
- Pain and distension of the abdomen.

GASTRIC DILATION & VOLVULUS (GDV)

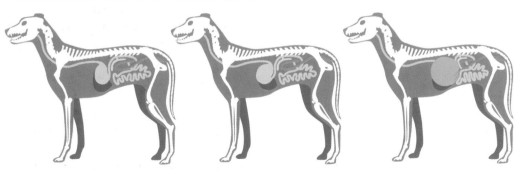

1. As the stomach swells (gastric dilation), it begins to twist (volvulus).

2. Rotation of the distended stomach can affect its blood supply and prevent it from emptying.

3. The distended stomach may fill the abdomen, putting pressure on other organs and tissues.

Diagnosis is possible after a simple examination, but X-rays are often needed to confirm stomach dilation and to help assess whether or not a twist is present. Affected dogs normally have severe circulatory problems when they are seen. The resulting shock can be more serious than their stomach swelling. Blood tests and even an ECG to check heart function may also be required. A drip is usually necessary in order to stabilize the circulation.

Treatment Temporary relief of stomach dilation may be achieved by releasing gas using a needle. If the stomach is not twisted – or only slightly twisted – it may be possible to pass a tube into the stomach through which fluid and gas can be removed.

Surgery is normally needed to reposition the stomach and spleen and to fix the stomach in place to try to prevent future episodes of GDV.

Because of the rapid course of this disease, many dogs are very ill by the time they are first seen, and even with appropriate treatment some do not survive. The sooner dogs are seen and treated appropriately, the better their chance of survival.

GASTRIC FOREIGN BODY

A foreign body, e.g., a stone or a part-chewed toy in the stomach, can cause a mechanical blockage in the outflow from the stomach.

Symptoms
- Vomiting.

How to prevent
GDV

GDV tends to occur in deep-chested, large-breed dogs (such as Mastiffs, Rottweilers, and Bernese Mountain Dogs) that are fed large meals, eat fast, and exercise close to their feeding time. To reduce the chance of this condition in predisposed dogs, never feed them within an hour of exercise; feed susceptible dogs two or three small meals daily; slow their eating by separating them from other dogs at feeding time and using toys in the food bowl or barrier bowls (bowls with only a small opening). Also, try to prevent them from drinking large amounts of water close to the time at which they eat.
Remember: GDV is an emergency. *Symptoms of attempting to vomit without success, panting, drooling, and abdominal swelling call for urgent veterinary attention.*

- Blockage may induce inflammation and cause pain, which can contribute to further vomiting.

Diagnosis may be possible following a clinical examination and palpation of the stomach region, but a barium meal followed by X-rays may be needed.

Treatment may involve surgical removal of the offending item. Although most dogs do very well after surgery, those that have severe disease in the stomach wall or are otherwise unwell may have ongoing problems.

PYLORIC STENOSIS

This involves physical narrowing of the tube out of the stomach. Emptying of the stomach becomes compromised. This problem can relate to a tumor in the outflow area of the stomach, inflammation of the stomach wall, or abnormal conformation of the stomach, a condition that is most common in small-breed dogs.

Symptoms

- Bouts of vomiting, particularly when the stomach is full.

Diagnosis involves a barium feed followed by X-rays of the stomach to visualize the narrowed area. Ultrasound scanning can also be helpful.

Treatment Depending on the cause, surgery may be needed to widen the affected tube. Alternatively, dogs may benefit from medical treatments to aid normal muscular movements in this area, as well as being fed a soft, moist diet.

GASTRITIS AND GASTRIC ULCERS

Symptoms

- Intermittent or recurrent symptoms of vomiting, regurgitation, and burping due to disease in the stomach.

What are

Barium X-rays

Barium X-rays, or "a barium series," involves feeding a dog food mixed with barium and then taking X-rays every fifteen to thirty minutes to trace the food moving through the body. It outlines the inside surface of the digestive tract, allowing this to be assessed. It also shows whether or not food is moving through the system overly fast or whether there are any blockages in the digestive system.

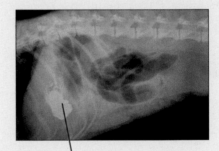

This X-ray taken after feeding the dog a barium meal clearly shows it within the stomach.

- Abnormal accumulation of bile in the stomach may contribute to inflammation of the stomach lining, which can cause vomiting. Similar symptoms may be caused by the presence of certain bacteria. Viral infections, intestinal parasites, and stomach wall tumors can also be involved. Affected dogs may vomit some blood and experience severe pain in the stomach area if a gastric ulcer forms.

Diagnosis may involve blood tests and X-rays, but endoscopic examination of the stomach lining is most helpful.

Treatment of dogs with acid-related inflammation may simply necessitate feeding several smaller meals a day and often one last thing at night to help prevent early morning vomiting when the stomach is empty. Other cases may need antacid medicines, pain-relieving medicines, anti-inflammatories, and worming treatments. Low-allergy diets may also be helpful in cases where stomach inflammation relates to food sensitivity.

Right: Small breeds of dog, such as this Jack Russell, are particularly prone to developing pyloric stenosis.

PYLORIC STENOSIS

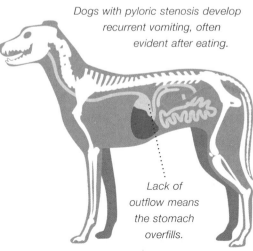

Dogs with pyloric stenosis develop recurrent vomiting, often evident after eating.

Lack of outflow means the stomach overfills.

Food enters the stomach through the esophagus sphincter.

A narrowing of the pylorus prevents outflow.

Pancreatic diseases

The pancreas is a gland that produces insulin (see page 120) and a number of enzymes involved in the digestion of fat, carbohydrates, and protein.

PANCREATITIS

Inflammation in the pancreas can occur as a sudden acute problem, particularly in overweight dogs on a high-fat diet or those that suddenly scavenge some fatty food. Certain antibiotics, anti-epileptic medicines, and diuretics can predispose dogs to pancreatitis. Some infections and parasites may also be contributory factors.

Symptoms

- Affected dogs develop pain in the front area of the abdomen so that they sometimes adopt the "praying" position, where they lie down at the front end but lift up their back legs to try to relieve their pain.
- The inflammation can be so severe that it damages the pancreas and other organs, makes the affected dog very weak, and induces severe vomiting.
- Other symptoms, relating to secondary problems in other parts of the body, include labored breathing and jaundice (page 84).

Diagnosis is based on blood tests that generally show an exceptionally high level of the enzymes amylase and lipase in the blood. Other enzymes and inflammatory chemicals may also increase. X-rays and ultrasound imaging of the pancreas may aid diagnosis. Examining a biopsy of the pancreas may be necessary.

Treatment involves giving intravenous fluids to rehydrate affected animals, as well as anti-vomiting medicines. In some cases, antibiotics and anti-inflammatory medicines may also be required. It may be necessary to withdraw food for several days while cases are stabilized.

Outcomes of pancreatitis are variable; some dogs suffer ongoing or repeated bouts of disease, although feeding a low-fat diet may help to avoid future problems.

EXOCRINE PANCREATIC INSUFFICIENCY

One of the roles of the pancreas is to produce the enzymes the body needs to digest fat. These enzymes pass from the pancreas into the duodenum, mix with the food particles in the bowel, and enable fat to be broken down so that it can be absorbed through the gut wall into the bloodstream. If the pancreas does not make sufficient amounts of the enzymes needed for fat digestion, the affected dog cannot absorb fat and loses it in feces. The fat that remains in the bowel blocks some of the water absorption from the food. This condition is hereditary in some breeds of dogs, but it can also follow pancreatic damage due to pancreatitis.

Symptoms

- Diarrhea.
- Affected dogs lose weight or maintain a very low weight because they cannot digest the fat in their diet.
- Dogs are usually very hungry.

Diagnosis involves taking blood tests to look at

What is
Ultrasound scanning

Ultrasound scanning uses differing resistance to sound to build up an image of soft tissues on a computer screen. It can be particularly helpful for looking at abdominal organs and bowel, allowing measurements of bowel wall thickness, and assessment of bowel structure. It is also helpful for examining the heart.

the levels of TLI (trypsin-like immunoreactivity) in the blood, which indicate whether or not the pancreas is producing fat-digesting enzymes. Other blood tests help with diagnosis.

Treatment necessitates feeding a low-fat diet, together with powdered pancreatic enzymes. This allows the fat in the food to be digested so that the dog can absorb the fat fragments, thus resolving the consequent diarrhea and allowing affected dogs to gain weight. Ongoing treatment is generally required.

Left: Belgian Sheepdogs, German Shepherd Dogs, Rough Collies, and English Setters can have an inherited form of pancreatic insufficiency.

Intestinal diseases

Diseases affecting the intestines often cause diarrhea, but where a blockage results, vomiting may also be a consequence.

INTESTINAL FOREIGN BODIES

Many dogs chew toys and eat parts of them, some chew or carry stones, and others steal their owner's clothing and belongings and eat those. Some foreign bodies lodge in the stomach, creating a partial obstruction and causing gastric inflammation and intermittent vomiting. However, others pass through the pylorus into the intestines. There, instead of causing a partial, intermittent obstruction (as in the stomach), the foreign body often becomes a sudden and complete obstruction. If the obstruction is sufficiently wide or the foreign body is sharp,

Some foreign bodies, such as this stone, are opaque to X-rays and show up well on the X-ray. This is the cause of the vomiting.

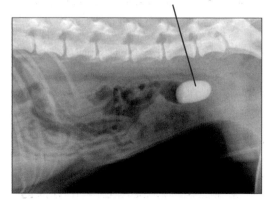

> ## ! Be aware
> ## *Foreign bodies*
>
> *Foreign bodies removed from dogs' stomachs and intestines include stones, bones, a baby's doll, fabric, balls and other toys, corn cobs, remote controls, cell phones, potato peelers, kitchen knives, and virtually anything else you can imagine! Puppies are much more likely than adults to eat inappropriate items, so monitor them with particular care.*

bowel wall damage can occur, which can rapidly cause shock, collapse, and even death.

Symptoms
- Acute onset of severe, recurrent vomiting.
- In many cases, affected animals are unable to even keep water down.
- Other symptoms relate to circulatory shock (due to damage to the bowel wall circulation) and dehydration.
- Affected dogs can rapidly become weak and unable to rise.

Diagnosis can be difficult, as dogs showing signs such as severe vomiting, dehydration, and weakness may be suffering from infectious **gastroenteritis.** The veterinarian may be able to feel the foreign body when palpating the dog's abdomen, but in many cases X-rays are needed to confirm diagnosis. Sometimes barium is fed first to show the inside surface of the bowel on X-rays. Ultrasound scanning may also be helpful. **Treatment** usually involves giving the dog an IV (intravenous) drip to maintain fluid levels and prevent dehydration. Foreign bodies that are too big to pass through or any that are sharp or otherwise likely to cause further damage need surgical removal. In some cases, damaged portions of the bowel may need to be removed. However, if foreign bodies appear small, inert, and rounded, regular meals of bulky foods, together with supportive medicines, may allow the foreign body to move through with minimum problems, thus avoiding surgery.

Most dogs rapidly regain full strength. However, damaged or surgically treated areas of bowel may become scarred or narrowed, or may develop adhesions to other areas of bowel. Some dogs, particularly those that have several episodes requiring surgery, may suffer ongoing digestive problems.

INTESTINAL TWIST / HERNIA / INTUSSUSCEPTION

Occasionally, a loop of bowel becomes twisted or passes through an opening, or hernia, in the body wall (sometimes found at the umbilicus, or belly button). Alternatively, one section of bowel may telescope into another piece of bowel (an intussusception). If this happens, the piece of gut can become constricted and its blood supply may be affected, leading to symptoms that are almost identical to those seen when a foreign body causes an obstruction.

INTUSSUSCEPTION

1. Intussusceptions are common in young puppies suffering from chronic diarrhea, often due to a poor diet or worms.

2. Over-contraction and inflammation of the bowel cause a section of bowel to constrict and its blood supply to be affected.

3. This area can pass into adjacent bowel, creating a blockage. Symptoms can progress from diarrhea to vomiting and collapse.

Symptoms
- Sudden copious vomiting.
- Dogs are usually unable to even keep water down. They dehydrate rapidly and may become weak and collapse.
- A swelling at a hernia site may be recognized if a hernia is present.

Diagnosis may necessitate X-rays or ultrasound scanning. In cases where a sudden swelling of an existing hernia is seen at the time when the symptoms develop, the diagnosis may be evident. Intussusceptions may cause a sausage-shaped swelling to form inside the dog, which may be palpable when the abdomen is examined.

Treatment involves emergency surgery to untwist or relocate the compromised section of bowel so that it can regain normal circulation and function. In some cases, where irreversible bowel damage has already occurred, a section of damaged bowel may also need to be removed. Intravenous fluids and treatment of pain and infection are also necessary.

GASTROENTERITIS AND ENTERITIS

These terms mean literally inflammation of the stomach and intestine or the intestine alone. Gastroenteritis can follow anything that causes inflammation in the digestive system.

Symptoms

- Vomiting (where the stomach is involved).
- Diarrhea (where the main problem is in the intestines).
- In most cases, both vomiting and diarrhea. Both can be severe and may contain blood.
- Dogs with a great deal of inflammation may temporarily lose bowel control, so that the diarrhea drips or gushes from them without them being able to stop it.

Diagnosis generally involves examining a fecal sample at a laboratory. The bacteria involved can be identified by culturing the sample. Other tests can identify viruses, such as parvovirus. Worms and other parasites can be identified by examination using a microscope.

Treatment is aimed at relieving the symptoms with medicines to slow gastrointestinal motility and, sometimes, to suppress vomiting. Affected

Above: *Elderly owners with suppressed immune systems should avoid contact with dogs suspected of carrying infectious gastroenteritis.*

dogs may also need oral electrolytes or even an intravenous drip to replace fluid and salt losses and prevent dehydration. The underlying problem will also need specific treatment. Antibiotics may be required if the dog is passing blood, and where a bacterial problem is identified. It may also be necessary to withhold food from affected dogs for twenty-four hours. After that, feed a very bland diet, such as one based on cooked chicken and rice. Normal food can be reintroduced gradually once the dog is better.

ENTERITIS AND COLITIS

Inflammation in the small intestine (enteritis) and the large bowel (colitis) may also be associated with allergies to food items, stress, low-grade bowel damage following parasite infestations, disorders in the balance of bacteria, and even cancerous thickening or infiltration of the bowel wall. Anything that reduces the ability of the body to reabsorb fluid and nutrients from the bowels can contribute to the following:

Symptoms

- Diarrhea, which may contain blood.
- Weight loss, thirst, and occasional vomiting. Affected dogs may lose so much weight that they become weak.
- Signs of abdominal pain.

Diagnosis may necessitate X-rays of the abdomen after feeding barium, which outlines the inner surface of the bowel. Ultrasound scanning and endoscopy may also allow imaging of the thickened bowel wall. Laboratory examination of biopsy samples of the bowel wall and associated lymph nodes may be needed.

Treatment may involve feeding a hypoallergenic diet, as well as probiotic supplements to try

Below: Children should observe careful hygiene to avoid catching infections from their dogs.

> **Be aware**
> ## Risk of infection
>
> *Many of the causes of vomiting and diarrhea are infectious.*
>
> - *Parvovirus is infectious to other dogs, so affected dogs should be isolated from other canines.*
> - *Salmonella, Campylobacter, and E. coli bacteria can be infectious to humans (zoonotic), so always observe very good hygiene when dealing with a dog suffering from diarrhea and/or vomiting. Any similar symptoms in humans should be dealt with promptly by a doctor. Young or elderly individuals, whether dogs or humans, are particularly susceptible to disease.*

to rebalance the "good bugs" in the digestive system. Antibiotics may be needed to treat any infection present. Medicines can slow the progress of food through the bowels to enable more to be absorbed. Other medicines can reduce inflammation in the bowel wall.

Outcome Some dogs do well on treatment, but most dogs with chronic inflammation in their bowel wall or with bowel wall damage following other diseases will have ongoing problems that, at best, will need ongoing treatment.

Intestinal worms

Worms and worm-related disease are common digestive problems. Although few dogs show external signs of worm-related problems, many have low-grade infestations that cause only mild disease. Treating dogs infested with intestinal parasites is important.

Symptoms

- Weight loss, vomiting, and diarrhea (which may contain worms).
- Excessive hunger.
- Long-term bowel disorders (which can be difficult to treat) may follow parasitic damage to the gut walls.

Diagnosis is relatively easy to achieve; any parasites present can be identified following laboratory examination of a fecal sample.

Treatments Various treatments are available, but regular preventative medicines are advisable in order to avoid disease (see page 21).

TAPEWORMS

Tapeworms *(Taenia, Echinococcus,* and *Dipylidium)* are widespread. Some types can affect humans. *Echinococcus multilocularis,* which is widespread in Europe and also found in the U.S. and other countries, is currently thought to be absent in the U.K. For this reason, one of the criteria for bringing dogs into the U.K. under the Pet Travel Scheme is that they be wormed with a product effective against this parasite before they enter the country. This is for their own benefit and in-contact humans.

Symptoms

- Diarrhea and vomiting.
- The passage from the anus of small egg sacs that resemble grains of rice.

Treatment Regular worming with an effective product at least once every three months will prevent disease.

ROUNDWORMS

Roundworms (e.g., *Toxocara canis*) are widespread, even though they are easy to prevent with regular worming. Many dogs are unwormed or inadequately wormed and shed roundworm eggs. These can be picked up from the ground and can infect other dogs and also people. In children, they can migrate through various organs and cause substantial disease.

Pregnant and lactating female dogs commonly suffer a reactivation of dormant roundworms in their bodies. These infect unborn and young puppies and can result in high levels of infection in young puppies.

Symptoms

- Diarrhea and vomiting.
- Dogs pass worms that resemble spaghetti.

Treatment Effective worming treatments may be needed as often as once a month.

HOOKWORMS

Hookworms such as *Ancylostoma* and *Uncinaria* are common in the U.S. and mainland Europe. They can also infect humans.

ROUNDWORM LIFE CYCLE

Infected dog passes larvae and eggs in feces.

Some larvae lie dormant until they are reactivated during pregnancy and pass to the puppies.

Toxacara eggs and larvae on grass and the ground are inadvertently eaten by dogs or children.

Children can be infected by contact with affected dogs or puppies or the environment.

Puppies can be born infected, or infected by their mother's milk.

Symptoms
- Damage done by their mouthparts causes diarrhea and weight loss.
- Intestinal hemorrhage.
- Blood loss and anemia.

Treatment Carry out preventative treatment using regular broad-spectrum wormers.

WHIPWORMS

Whipworms (*Trichuris vulpis*) are relatively common in the U.S. and mainland Europe. Like the other intestinal worms, they may cause few symptoms but can be involved in causing bowel wall damage, diarrhea, and electrolyte losses. Regular worming with an effective broad-spectrum product every three months should prevent disease.

OTHER PARASITIC AND PROTOZOAN DISEASES

Coccidia, Cryptosporidia, Giardia, and *Helicobacter* can cause symptoms of vomiting and diarrhea and may need treatment. Some may also be transmissible to humans; take care with hygiene when dealing with affected dogs.

Constipation, straining, and anal problems

Constipation and tenesmus (straining to pass feces) are common problems in older dogs, which tend to experience reduced gut function as they age. This is due to a combination of factors, such as less exercising, eating less, and having less active organs. Any issues that increase water losses elsewhere in the body, such as kidney disease or even just hot weather, can make feces drier and harder to pass. Conditions that narrow the colon, rectum, or anus can also contribute to difficulty defecating.

Prostate problems can cause narrowing of the bowel in the colon and rectum. Bowel or

---

How to treat
Anal problems

Many anal tumors are benign and slow-growing. Some relate to high hormone levels in unneutered males and shrink down or stop growing if affected dogs are castrated. Those masses that interfere with defecation may require surgical removal.

Anal sac blockage or infection can result in anal pain and problems passing feces. In affected dogs the anal sacs may need to be emptied by squeezing, or even flushed under anesthesia or surgically removed.

ANAL SACS

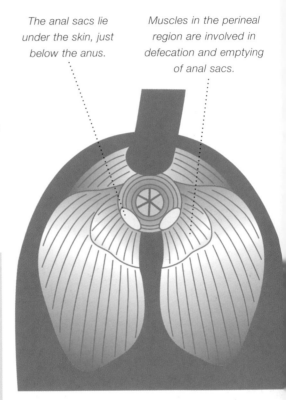

The anal sacs lie under the skin, just below the anus.

Muscles in the perineal region are involved in defecation and emptying of anal sacs.

anal tumors or anal gland infections may also reduce the width of the bowel and cause pain on defecation.

Symptoms
- Some dogs suffer muscle degeneration around the anal area, leading to the formation of perineal hernias (bulges of the bowel wall just

behind the anus). These can cause pocketing of feces, preventing them from being passed normally and resulting in further pressure on muscles in the area and further damage.

- Dogs affected by mobility problems and stiffness in the back and hips may find it hard to squat comfortably while defecating, which can also contribute to difficulty passing feces.

Diagnosis of problems in the anal area may require the veterinarian to perform a rectal examination with a gloved finger to feel the inner surface of the rectum and anus. The dog may have to be anesthetized or sedated, especially if further tests, such as X-rays, are needed to diagnose any abnormalities in this area. Any masses present may be sampled and submitted for laboratory examination for identification.

Above: Prolonged squatting and straining (tenesmus) may indicate anal or rectal problems.

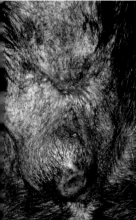

Left: Swelling and infection in the perineal area can indicate anal sac infection or tumors.

Treatments vary depending on the cause of the problem. Most senior foods contain increased levels of fiber, which helps bulk up feces and make them pass through more easily. Some old dogs also benefit from laxatives to aid the passage of feces. Some need pain relief and anti-inflammatory medicines to improve their mobility sufficiently so that they can squat normally. Surgical treatments may be needed to remove any masses that are present or to resolve perineal hernias and reestablish normal bowel function. In some cases, chronically infected anal sacs may need to be removed surgically.

Liver disease

Symptoms of liver (hepatic) disease vary enormously, reflecting the range of different functions of the organ. The liver is amazingly good at continuing to function, even when damaged. Symptoms of liver disease may not become evident until more than seventy percent of the liver has been affected. This means that by the time liver symptoms are recognized and a diagnosis is made, any disease process may have progressed so far that it is hard or even impossible to treat.

Symptoms

- Increased drinking.
- Loss of appetite.
- Weight loss.
- Restlessness, malaise, and lethargy.
- Vomiting, diarrhea, and abdominal swelling.
- Wobbliness and head pressing if toxin levels rise and affect brain function.
- Jaundice, or yellowing of the mucus membranes and skin.

HOW THE LIVER WORKS

Toxins in the body are filtered out by the liver and excreted.

Blood-clotting factors and immune products are produced.

Food products are broken down, glucose is stored, and other nutrients and vitamins are produced.

Bile produced by the liver aids digestion of foods in the intestines.

The liver makes bile from the damaged red blood cells it removes from the circulation.

Some of the liver's blood supply comes straight from the bowel, carrying nutrient products of food digestion, such as carbohydrates, proteins, and fats.

Bile is stored in the gall bladder, from where it flows via the bile duct into the duodenum, or small intestine, to enable fat digestion.

What does it do
The liver

In the liver, carbohydrates are stored as easily available sugar for quick energy release. Proteins are broken down to their constituent amino acids and reformed into chemicals the body needs. These range from enzymes to clotting factors (these enable blood to clot when wounds occur) and some kinds of hormones. Fats are also broken down within the liver for energy release, and cholesterol is made to control fat levels. In addition, the liver is a key organ in the breakdown and removal of toxins from the blood.

LOCATION OF THE LIVER

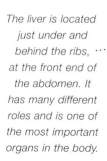
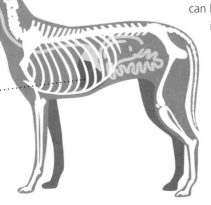

The liver is located just under and behind the ribs, at the front end of the abdomen. It has many different roles and is one of the most important organs in the body.

- Reduced levels of clotting factors made by the liver can result in affected dogs being particularly vulnerable to blood loss.
- Dogs with hepatitis may also show marked abdominal pain and have swelling of the abdomen due to an enlarged liver or the release of fluid (known as ascites) caused by the damaged liver.

Diagnosis

- A full clinical examination may identify symptoms of liver disease, but further tests are usually needed to confirm this, as well as to try to identify the exact type of disease involved.
- Blood tests can identify enzymes that indicate liver damage or that the liver is struggling to function. They may also show low urea levels and low glucose levels, which can relate to poor liver function. Special blood tests can detect raised ammonia levels and increased amounts of bile acids in the blood, which increase after a fatty meal. Further blood tests can be carried out if **Cushing's disease** is suspected as the cause of the liver disorder.
- Ultrasound scanning and X-rays may provide images that show the size and shape of the liver and its internal structure. Ultrasound can also be used to guide a biopsy needle into any suspicious areas to retrieve samples for analysis.

Treatments

Treating liver disease is complicated by the degree of damage that may be present by the time a diagnosis is made. In some cases a complete cure of liver disease is possible, but often, the best that can be hoped for is to stop or slow a disease process within the liver and reduce its workload, so that it can better cope with its functions. This may resolve the symptoms of disease.

- Dogs that experience an acute onset of severe liver disease may need hospital treatment on an intravenous drip to keep them hydrated and help flush toxins through the system. Other medicines may be needed, such as anti-inflammatory medications and antibiotics to treat infection.

Above: Small-breed dogs, such as this Yorkshire Terrier, are particularly prone to suffering from portosystemic shunt.

Left: Blue-green algal blooms cause discoloration of ponds and lakes and contain toxins that can cause liver disease.

PORTOSYSTEMIC SHUNT TYPES

In the normal dog, blood diffuses through the liver tissue, allowing vital functions to occur.

Intrahepatic shunt

This type of shunt carries blood through the liver without diffusing into the tissue.

Extrahepatic shunt

Here, the shunt involves blood bypassing the liver completely.

- Unless secondary neurological symptoms necessitate reducing the protein levels in food, dogs with liver disease benefit from a diet with sufficient protein levels to maintain muscle strength in an easily digestible, high-quality form. B vitamin supplementation may be required. Ursodeoxycholic acid, which helps stimulate bile flow, may also help support liver function, and there is some good evidence that food supplements containing S-adenosylmethionine (sAME) can be helpful.

PORTOSYSTEMIC SHUNT

Liver disease in young dogs is fairly rare, but there is one major condition seen relatively commonly in young dogs, particularly small and toy breeds. Portosystemic shunt relates to a developmental malformation of the blood vessels that supply the liver. A blood vessel that bypasses the liver in the womb during pregnancy should close off after birth. If it does not close off properly, some blood continues to bypass the liver in the young puppy, resulting in poor liver function.

Symptoms
- Slow growth, poor weight gain, and poor muscle development.
- Seizures or even coma (sometimes).
- Lethargy, increased drinking, and jaundice.

Diagnosis is possible following a range of blood tests that show poor liver function, combined with ultrasound scanning of the liver to identify the abnormal blood vessel.

Treatment In some cases it is possible to close off this blood vessel surgically. This can result in blood flow being directed back through the liver in normal vessels, with a consequent improvement in liver function. Such dogs may be able to go on to lead a normal life, with relatively little ongoing treatment or monitoring. In other cases, surgery may not be possible or is only partially successful, and ongoing medication may be needed.

TOXIC DISEASES

A number of diseases can cause liver damage due to the accumulation of toxins. This can follow abnormal metabolism of certain nutrients in some dogs. (Certain breeds are prone to

? What can Blood tests reveal

Blood can be tested for a range of enzymes, cells, and salts, as well as specific hormones and other chemicals, such as toxins. Routine blood tests usually include:

- A full blood count (hematology) to test levels of red blood cells, white blood cells, and platelets.
- A biochemistry screen to look at enzymes relating to liver, kidney, bowel, bone, and muscle function, as well as protein levels and glucose (which can indicate diabetes mellitus).
- Electrolyte levels (the major salts needed for normal cell function, and muscle and heart contraction).

accumulation of copper in the liver, which causes liver damage.) Poisons such as acetaminophen and ibuprofen (these human medicines should not be used in dogs) and blue-green algal toxins (in ponds) can also cause liver damage, as can chemicals containing chlorinated carbon, tannic acid, and selenium.

Symptoms
- Previously healthy dogs suddenly become affected by symptoms of liver disease.

Diagnosis Blood tests reveal evidence of acute hepatic disease. Identifying the cause of the problem may be trickier unless, for example, an episode of poisoning has been evident.

Treatment Initially, this is based on hydrating the affected animal with intravenous fluids to help flush out toxins, and giving medicines to support the liver and help it function. In the long term, dogs that suffer from copper sensitivity may need a special low-copper diet.

Liver infection

Infection of the liver can cause acute liver disease that mimics toxic liver disease described above. Infection may develop in the liver from bacteria or viruses in the circulation, or it may occur following a spread of infection from the bowel **(enteritis)**, passing to the liver via the portal vein or bile duct.

Symptoms
- Vomiting, collapse, abdominal pain, and seizures.

Diagnosis Liver disease can be diagnosed

following blood tests. Further tests may be needed to identify any infectious disease that is present. Leptospirosis, adenovirus, and canine herpes virus can all cause acute onset liver disease, as can *Campylobacter, Salmonella, Clostridium,* and *Bacillus* bacteria. Toxoplasmosis and fungal histoplasmosis (other types of infection) may also be involved. *Salmonella, Campylobacter,* toxoplasmosis, and even leptospirosis can all be zoonotic, meaning they are transmissible to humans.

LEPTOSPIROSIS

Dogs may develop leptospirosis after contact with urine from an infected rat, from wildlife, from livestock, or from another dog.

Above: Direct contact between dogs can allow transmission of a wide range of infections.

Symptoms
- Fever, vomiting, dehydration, and jaundice; in unvaccinated dogs this can progress to death within as little as one or two days. Milder disease may be seen in vaccinated dogs.
- In severe cases, muscle weakness and pain, vomiting and diarrhea, dehydration, leakage of blood from blood vessels to cause bruising, and **kidney disease**.

Treatment If affected dogs are to have a chance of survival, they usually need appropriate antibiotics, intravenous fluid therapy, and, in some cases, blood transfusions.

ADENOVIRAL HEPATITIS

Canine adenovirus can cause **respiratory disease** and coughing but can also be responsible for severe liver disease and **kidney disease**. Eye inflammation may also occur, causing the eyes to develop a bluish tinge. Sudden death may be the first sign of disease.

Symptoms

- Vomiting, diarrhea.
- Coughing, seizures.
- Weakness and "blue eye."

What is
Peritonitis

Peritonitis occurs when the abdomen lining becomes inflamed and infected. This can follow bowel leakage from intestinal injury or disease, or can be a consequence of disease in other abdominal organs, such as the liver, pancreas, spleen, or kidneys. Severe peritonitis can cause abdominal pain, weakness due to problems with blood circulation, and vomiting and diarrhea. Diagnosis may involve blood tests and tests on fluid samples from the abdominal cavity. Surgical treatment may be needed to treat any underlying organ disease. Antibiotics and anti-inflammatory medicines may be required.

Treatment Fluids, anti-inflammatory medicines, and hyperimmune serum (medication containing antibodies) can all aid recovery. However, vaccination is far preferable. Vaccination can prevent leptospirosis and adenoviral hepatitis. Sadly, dogs die every year as a consequence of these preventable diseases.

Other causes of acute liver disease

Liver disease can also occur as a secondary consequence of **anemia**, hemolysis (blood cell breakdown), heat stroke, bowel disease, **pancreatitis**, and **trauma**. Any of these conditions can progress over time and cause chronic liver disease if not treated successfully.

TRAUMA

Trauma, or injury, can cause liver damage and consequent disease. Falls from up high, impacts due to road traffic accidents, or other hard blows to the abdomen are all potential causes of injury. It may be obvious that a dog has suffered trauma; the owner may have witnessed an injury. However, sometimes dogs suffer an injury out on a walk without the owner being aware of it.

Symptoms

- Skin damage and bruising.
- The liver may become bruised, develop a hematoma (blood blister under its capsule), or may even rupture, leaking blood, damaged tissue, and even bile into the abdominal cavity.
- Peritonitis may result.

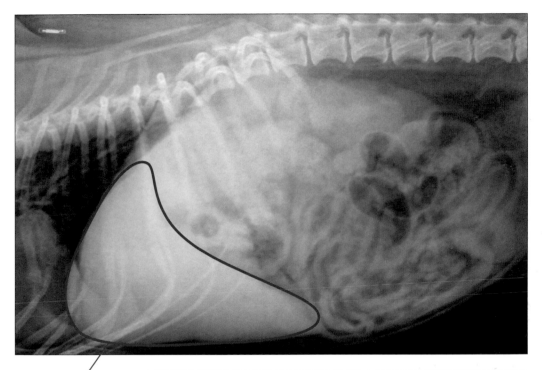

An enlarged liver may be detected with X-rays; the liver shadow extends far beyond the edge of the rib cage.

Right: Dogs that are unwell may be miserable, lethargic, and weak.

- Weakness and even collapse and inability to stand due to circulatory problems.
- Severe abdominal pain may be apparent.
- A change in the normal contour of the body due to damaged ribs or abdominal muscle injury.

Diagnosis of exactly what injuries or damage are present necessitates blood tests to assess liver function. X-rays and ultrasound scanning can be used to assess the contour of the liver and its internal structure.

Treatment Dogs with severe bruising may heal and recover if rested and treated with supportive medicines and feeding. However, more severe injuries may require emergency surgery, perhaps at a referral hospital.

Liver tumors

Tumors can develop in the liver, either following spread from cancer elsewhere in the body or as primary lesions. They can cause disease both by damaging the liver and affecting its function, and also by virtue of the space they take up in the abdomen.

Symptoms
- Vomiting, diarrhea.
- Weight loss and abdominal pain.
- Neurological symptoms (possibly).
- Anemia.
- Obvious abdominal swelling (possibly).

Diagnosis of the presence of a tumor may be aided by blood tests, but X-rays and ultrasound scanning are also useful diagnostic procedures,

> **?**
>
> *What is*
> ## MRI scanning
>
> *MRI scanning involves imaging an area within a magnetic field and measuring the response of the tissues to radio wave pulses. The computer-generated image reflects the water content in different tissues and can provide astonishing detail, particularly of soft tissues.*

as they may allow identification of an enlarged liver and possibly of the tumor within the normal structure of the liver. In order to identify the type of tumor present, a biopsy of the tissue is needed. This may be done surgically under general anaesthesia or by using a biopsy needle directed through the skin, guided by ultrasound scanning. However, the liver can bleed excessively after a biopsy, and dogs with clotting disorders as a consequence of their liver disease may not be able to cope with a biopsy sample being taken.

Treatment may involve removing the tumor and part of the liver in some cases, but this is tricky surgery and may necessitate referral to a specialist center. Some kinds of liver tumors **(lymphoma)** respond well to chemotherapy. Others may not be treatable, or the only treatment possible may be to use steroids to try to slow their growth.

Chronic liver disease

Chronic, or longer term, low-grade liver disease can occur as a consequence of ongoing acute disease that has not been controlled with treatments. Alternatively, it may occur following low-grade liver damage, infection, inflammatory disease, exposure to toxins, or tumor development.

Symptoms

- Weight loss and vomiting.
- Weakness and increased drinking.
- Neurological symptoms of hepatic encephalopathy (possibly).

Diagnosis Blood test results can be evaluated to diagnose the exact cause of disease, together with ultrasound scans and other data from CT or MRI scans.

Treatment Ultimately, these diseases are rarely responsive to treatment. In most cases, the best that can be achieved is to support the function of the ailing liver with an appropriate diet and food supplements.

> *What is*
> ## *CT scanning*
>
> *CT scanning uses a specialized radiography machine to take a series of image "slices" through the area under examination. These can be viewed on a computer and processed to form a three-dimensional image.*

In cases of severe or long-standing liver disease, levels of toxins in the blood may rise to the point where they cross the blood/brain barrier and pass into the brain, resulting in changes in brain function. Wobbliness, weakness, poor coordination, and depression are common symptoms of this condition, known as hepatic encephalopathy, but another is that affected dogs often start to head press (they stand in a corner pressing their head against the wall) as a response to head pain.

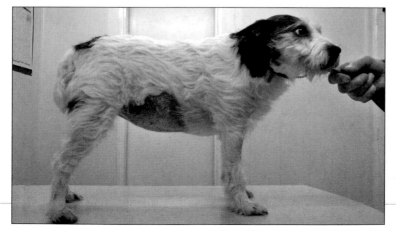

Left: *Liver enlargement can cause a "pot-bellied" appearance due to enlargement of the abdomen. Some dogs with liver disease develop secondary changes in the skin, with ulceration and crusting of the feet, muzzle, anal area, and ear tips.*

Disease of the kidneys and urinary system

Symptoms of urinary diseases can be varied.

Symptoms

- For many dogs, the first sign is that they may drink more, urinate more, and perhaps start to have urinary accidents.
- As kidney (renal) disease progresses, the kidneys may shut down and the dog stops drinking and urinating. These symptoms can be even more serious and require emergency treatment.
- Leakage of salts, nutrients, and protein into the urine by the diseased kidney contributes to water loss, causing affected dogs to lose weight and suffer muscle wastage and weakness, as well as to urinate excessively.
- Appetite may be reduced. As a result of increased fluid losses, affected dogs need to drink more.
- Kidney disease can also cause **anemia** and bone weakness due to calcium disorders. It can lead to an increase in toxin levels in the blood; if toxins cross the blood/brain barrier into the brain, neurological symptoms result, such as wobbliness, **seizures**, and even collapse and coma.
- Mouth ulceration and halitosis.
- Dogs with urinary disease, especially those with kidney or bladder infections, tumors, or stones, may also experience abdominal pain.
- Bladder diseases may cause incontinence, and both bladder and kidney disease can cause dogs to pass discolored urine or blood in their urine, which their owners may notice.

Diagnosis

The signs seen by owners and picked up at initial examination by a veterinarian may suggest kidney disease, but further tests are needed to diagnose the problem exactly.

- Urine tests allow the veterinarian to assess the levels of blood, protein, and other substances in the urine, which can provide a great deal of information about the healthiness of the urinary system.

? What do they do
The kidneys

The main role of the kidneys is to regulate the amount of fluid and salts in the body by controlling how much of them passes out of the body in urine and how much is reabsorbed and recycled back into the circulation. The kidneys filter toxins out of the blood and release them into the urine. They also manufacture chemicals needed for the formation of red blood cells and are involved in maintaining calcium and vitamin D levels in the body.

- Measuring the specific gravity of urine reveals how concentrated it is, which indicates how well the kidneys are working. Diseased kidneys may lose the ability to reabsorb water and concentrate the urine. In addition, microscopic examination of urine can help identify any crystals or stones present.
- Blood tests may show raised levels of urea and creatinine, chemicals excreted by normal kidneys. Further specific blood tests may provide more detailed information.
- Ultrasound scanning of the kidneys can provide a detailed image of the internal structure and may allow damaged or diseased areas to be identified.
- X-rays of the abdomen can image the position and outline of the kidneys. Ultrasound scanning is also very useful when investigating bladder disease, as it allows an image of the bladder and its contents to be examined. Bladder X-rays may also be useful, sometimes incorporating a technique in which the bladder is filled with air or dye so that it shows up more clearly on the X-rays.

LOCATION OF THE KIDNEYS

The kidneys are positioned toward the front end of the abdomen; they are tucked up under the spine and are also protected by the upper part of the ribs.

Urine collects in the kidneys and then passes down the ureters to the bladder.

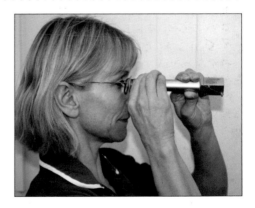

Urine is held in place by the bladder sphincter, until the dog has the opportunity to void it via the urethra.

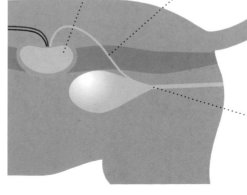

Above: *Urine tests, such as checking specific gravity with a refractometer, can help identify kidney and bladder diseases.*

Treatments

- For kidney diseases, intravenous fluid therapy is often required to flush out toxins from the system and maintain a normal circulation.
- Infections are treated with antibiotics.
- Pain relief may be needed in many conditions, although any medicines excreted through the kidneys should only be used with care.
- Surgical treatment may be required to remove kidney or bladder stones; to remove kidney or bladder tumors; or to repair injured parts of the urinary system.

Specific diets may help dogs with urinary diseases. For kidney disease, highly palatable and easily digestible diets that combine controlled levels of high-quality protein, increased levels of vitamins B, D, and E, low salt levels, and reduced levels of phosphate help to reduce the workload of the kidneys. Phosphate binders may also be used to reduce phosphate and help prevent calcium disorders and bone weakening.

Dogs with crystals or stones in the urinary system may also benefit from special diets that help prevent minerals from crystalizing in urine or that aid the breakdown of crystals and stones. To establish the appropriate prescription diet, it is important to know what stone type is present, so identifying the type of crystals present in the urine is the first step.

Other treatments for urinary problems include medicines that increase bladder sphincter tone to aid control of urinary incontinence.

Many types of urinary disease are treatable; some can be cured, but for others the best that can be achieved is reducing the workload of the urinary system and aiming to slow the progression of disease.

Kidney disease in puppies

Although most kidney diseases are seen in old age, young puppies can suffer from kidney disorders if they have malformed or abnormal kidneys. Dogs are sometimes born with only one kidney or with fused abnormal kidneys. Sometimes cysts form in the kidneys of young dogs that can affect kidney function.

> **?** *What can*
> ## Urine tests reveal
>
> *Urine can be tested for a range of different products of digestion, including protein and glucose as well as the presence of red or white blood cells, tumor cells, or even some types of cancer cells. Under a microscope, cells and any crystals present can be identified more accurately. Tests also indicate how well the kidneys are working to concentrate urine and can reveal early signs of liver disease, kidney disease, diabetes mellitus, and bladder or prostate disease.*

Symptoms
- Poor growth and slow weight gain.
- Excessive drinking (although this may not be easy to recognize). Affected puppies are often difficult to house train as a consequence.

Diagnosis may necessitate a combination of blood tests, X-rays, and ultrasound scanning.

Treatment Although specific treatment may be possible in some cases, many affected puppies cannot be cured. However, they do benefit from appropriate diets and supplements that reduce the workload of the kidneys as much as possible, thereby helping them lead the healthiest possible lives.

Acute kidney disease

Acute renal failure can occur in previously healthy dogs following toxic damage to the kidneys or in the presence of certain infections, including **leptospirosis**. Toxins, such as ethylene glycol **(antifreeze)**, paraquat (a weed-killer) and even certain medicines (in susceptible dogs), can cause sudden onset kidney damage. Lack of circulation due to a blood clot, or inflammatory disease of the blood vessels can also cause

acute renal failure, as can sudden dehydration due to lack of water, or urinary blockage (for example, due to **urolithiasis** or **trauma**), which causes back pressure that damages the kidneys.

Symptoms
- Increased drinking and urine production, but affected dogs may progress straight to the stage where renal shutdown occurs and they virtually stop drinking and urinating.
- Vomiting, diarrhea, loss of appetite.
- Dehydration and collapse.

Left: Healthy puppies are naturally inquisitive and may eat poisons, causing disease.

- Over a few days, affected dogs may develop mouth ulcers, become anemic, and can even develop seizures.

Diagnosis Urine and blood tests may show raised urea and creatinine levels, and anemia may also be evident. (Creatinine is broken down from creatine, an energy storage compound.)

Treatment can include intravenous fluids and medicines that aid renal function.

Chronic kidney disease

Chronic renal failure occurs when low-grade damage to the kidney takes place over a long period of time, causing a gradual onset of kidney disease. There are a number of reasons for this. Affected dogs may have genetic or acquired diseases that damage the kidney's tissues, or they may sustain kidney damage due to low-grade infections or following an episode of acute renal failure. Chronic kidney failure may also be a consequence of old age deterioration and can follow the development of kidney tumors.

AMYLOIDOSIS, GLOMERULONEPHROPATHY, AND FANCONI'S SYNDROME

Abnormal metabolism in some dogs can lead to protein particles being deposited in certain organs (amyloidosis). When deposited in the kidney, protein and amyloid particles cause a slow onset kidney damage that gradually affects the kidneys' ability to function. Similar problems occur in Fanconi's syndrome, glomerulonephropathy, and nephrotic syndrome, all of which involve gradual deterioration of the cells in the kidney and a slow progression of signs of disease.

Symptoms
- Increased drinking and increased urination.
- Loss of appetite, weight loss.
- Vomiting and diarrhea.
- Mouth ulceration.

Left: Increased drinking may be a sign of kidney disease. Getting to know your dog's usual routine will alert you to any significant increase in water intake.

- Affected dogs may become anemic due to reduced production of red blood cells. They may develop osteoporosis and suffer bone damage due to abnormal calcium metabolism.
- **Neurological disease** may also be seen because toxin levels in the blood rise as the affected dog's kidneys deteriorate.

Diagnosis Blood tests show raised urea and creatinine levels. In amyloidosis, very high levels of protein may be detected in the urine. X-rays and ultrasound scanning may reveal the kidneys to be shrunken and to contain abnormal tissue. Exact diagnosis necessitates laboratory examination of a biopsy sample.

Treatment Treating chronic renal disease is difficult and not particularly successful. However, some medical treatments are available and are aimed at reducing further damage or assisting the kidneys to function as normally as possible.

Renal diets can also assist affected dogs to stay as healthy as possible.

Urinary damage: trauma

Damage to the kidneys, ureters, or bladder can occur as a result of road traffic accidents, falls from up high, or injuries.

Symptoms

- Bruising of the kidneys or bladder can cause abdominal pain and the passing of blood in the urine.
- Symptoms of kidney failure may also occur.
- Urine leaking into the body cavity, leading to peritonitis as well as urinary disease.

! *Be aware*
Antifreeze

Ethylene glycol, the most common antifreeze, is surprisingly palatable to pets. It is extremely toxic and releases chemicals that cause neurological signs, such as incoordination and seizures, within hours. It also causes crystals to form in the kidneys and can result in kidney failure and death within a few days. In the early stages, symptoms may include breathlessness and increased drinking, but affected dogs become very collapsed as their kidneys shut down. They can become comatose.

Treatment is rarely successful, as owners are often unaware that their dog has consumed ethylene glycol and rarely bring them to the veterinarian promptly enough. However, intensive fluid therapy and medication may save dogs treated appropriately within the first few hours after they drink the ethylene glycol.

Diagnosis If an injury has been witnessed, kidney and bladder damage may be easy to diagnose. However, injuries can occur without the owner knowing, and in these cases diagnosing the exact problem is more difficult.

Blood tests and ultrasound scanning can identify the degree of any damage present.

Treatment Although mild injuries may heal on their own with rest and supportive medicines, surgical treatment may be required if any of the urinary structures have ruptured.

Urolithiasis

Some dogs have the tendency to precipitate mineral crystals in their urine, which can coalesce to form kidney stones or, more commonly, bladder stones. This may happen when dogs are fed a high-mineral diet or drink water high in minerals. It may be caused by a disorder in their metabolism that prevents normal breakdown of certain nutrients. For example, Dalmatians may have a hereditary condition that causes them to precipitate urate crystals. Other dogs may form struvite or calcium oxalate crystals. Crystals may also form as a consequence of chronic low-grade inflammation or infection in the urinary system.

Symptoms

- Stones developing in the kidneys or bladder may cause the affected dog to show signs of abdominal pain. However, sometimes no pain is apparent and very few signs are seen.
- The presence of stones may cause inflammation and irritation of the urinary tissues. Blood may be detected in the urine.
- If stones or stone fragments pass into the urethra they may cause a blockage. The first symptoms may be that the dog attempts and strains to urinate without success. This can be an emergency, because urine continues to be formed. Without treatment, the bladder can become over-full and may be damaged or even burst.

Diagnosis X-rays and ultrasound scanning allow identification of uroliths (stones). Blood tests may also be helpful.

Treatment may necessitate emergency surgery to remove stones and allow urine to be voided. In some cases, a catheter may be passed to allow stone fragments to be flushed out.

Right: Some Dalmatians are prone to developing urolithiasis. Once the condition is diagnosed, treatment may involve surgery and a special diet.

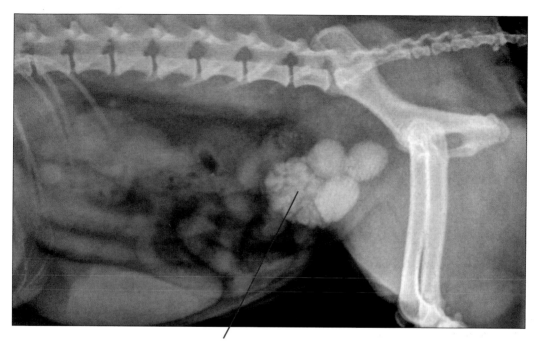

Multiple stones are clearly visible in the bladder on this X-ray. This is a serious condition that requires emergency surgery to remove them.

Dogs with small stones and stone fragments may respond to a special diet that helps dissolve stones and crystals and prevent their formation in the future by changing the acidity and the mineral content of the urine. The constitutents of this diet depend on the type of stone present.

Once diagnosed and stable on treatment, most dogs with urolithiasis do well, as long as they keep to their special diet and are checked out promptly if signs of urinary difficulties occur.

Cystitis and pyelonephritis

Kidney and bladder infections can build up after bacteria pass into these areas via the bloodstream or, particularly in female dogs (which have a shorter urethra that presents less of a barrier), they can be sucked into the bladder by pressure changes that occur after urination. Cystitis is very common.

Symptoms

• Affected dogs commonly start to pass urine more frequently and more urgently.

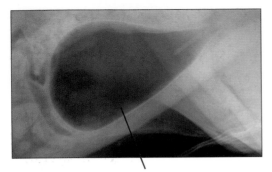

Filling the bladder with air allows the inner surface to be seen more clearly on the X-ray.

Accidents may occur if they do not get outside quickly.

- Although cystitis rarely makes dogs feel ill in themselves, they may show signs of pain when urinating and may pass discolored or bloody urine.
- Pyelonephritis, or kidney infection, can cause similar symptoms, but more often these infections cause affected dogs to develop a temperature and become depressed, lethargic, and unwell.

Diagnosis of urinary infections involves culturing urine samples at a laboratory in order to identify the bacteria present. For accurate results, samples may need to be uncontaminated (i.e., not voided via the urethra). This means obtaining the sample directly from the bladder by catheterization, which may involve anesthesia. Urine tests showing the presence of bacteria and red and white blood cells also indicate urinary infection.

Treatment with antibiotics usually results in a swift resolution of infection and the symptoms involved. In addition, dogs may need pain relief and anti-inflammatory medication.

Urinary incontinence

Urinary incontinence may occur if the bladder sphincter muscles are unable to close fully and hold urine within the bladder. This can occur in a condition called USMI, or urethral sphincter mechanism incompetence. It is generally seen in older, spayed female dogs and relates to a reduction in estrogen in the body, which results in the bladder sphincter becoming less effective.

Symptoms

- Affected female dogs pass urine without being aware of doing so, often when they are asleep, but they may also drip urine when awake.

Diagnosis can be achieved by checking a urine sample and ruling out other causes of apparent incontinence, such as cystitis or urolithiasis. X-rays of the abdomen may show the bladder sphincter to be widened and that the bladder occupies an abnormal position in the abdomen.

Treatment generally involves medicines that help the bladder sphincter muscle tighten. These usually work well and the problem resolves quickly, although ongoing treatment is generally required. Some dogs may need bladder surgery.

OTHER CAUSES OF INCONTINENCE

Malformations of the urinary system can cause abnormal urination. Sometimes the ureters enter the bladder too far back, so that the urine they pass into the bladder is poorly controlled by the bladder sphincter. This is seen in certain breeds such as Golden Retrievers, is associated with a hereditary condition, and is known as ectopic ureter syndrome.

Symptoms

• Affected puppies drip urine without knowing and are unable to control the passage of urine.

Diagnosis may necessitate specialized X-rays or ultrasound scanning to identify the position at which the ureters enter the bladder.

Below: Ectopic or malformed ureters may cause urinary incontinence in Golden Retriever puppies.

Treatment Affected puppies generally need surgical treatment to move the ureteral opening to a better position in the bladder wall.

Tumors

Kidney and bladder tumors are not uncommon.

Symptoms

• Abdominal pain.

• Abnormalities in urination (which may include incontinence), pain, on urination.

• The passage of blood in the urine.

Diagnosis Ultrasound scanning or X-rays may allow any tumors to be imaged, and blood tests and urine tests may be needed to assess their impact.

Treatment Surgical removal may be possible depending on the tumor type. Chemotherapy may also be an option.

The reproductive system

Female hormones produced by the ovaries result in several eggs maturing together every six months or so, when the female dog comes into estrus (season/heat, see page 38). If the female is mated, the eggs can be fertilized and a pregnancy may result (see page 42). If not, the estrus is followed by a period of time during which the uterus regresses, with a reduction in blood supply and hormonal levels, until the next season develops. In the unneutered male, sperm and hormones are continually produced, and mating can take place if there is contact with a female in estrus.

Symptoms

Symptoms of disease in the reproductive system are variable and often vague, so that it can be difficult to determine the exact problem exactly.

- Urinary discoloration or a discharge from the vulva or penis (possibly).
- Swelling of the abdomen or the testicles (possibly).
- Difficulty passing urine or feces (possibly).
- Infections can cause increased drinking, loss of appetite, vomiting, abdominal pain, breathlessness, and malaise.

Diagnosis

A thorough examination may reveal the cause of disease, but further tests are usually required.
- Urine and blood tests to exclude a range of other diseases, or to reveal raised white blood cell levels, indicating the presence of infection.
- Analyzing samples of prostatic fluid to show the cell types present can help diagnose tumors or infection in the prostate.
- X-rays and ultrasound scanning are often the most useful techniques, allowing imaging of the ovaries and uterus in the female or the prostate and bladder in the male.
- Vaginal swabs can be taken to allow infections to be identified or cells present to be analyzed.

Treatments

Treatments vary depending on the cause of disease. In many cases, removing elements of the dog's reproductive system may be curative or, because this results in decreased levels of the hormones that trigger diseases, may assist in the management of reproductive diseases.

Female reproductive diseases

A number of conditions relating to their hormonal systems can affect females. Many are solved or prevented by neutering.

PYOMETRA

This bacterial infection in the uterus is a very serious and potentially life-threatening condition. It is seen in mature, unneutered female dogs and becomes more common with age. The infection usually enters the uterus when the cervix is open

THE REPRODUCTIVE ORGANS

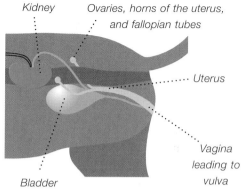

Kidney
Ovaries, horns of the uterus, and fallopian tubes
Uterus
Vagina leading to vulva
Bladder

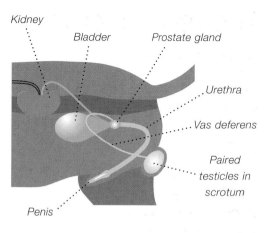

Kidney
Bladder
Prostate gland
Urethra
Vas deferens
Paired testicles in scrotum
Penis

Female reproductive system

The reproductive system in the female consists of ovaries, located just behind the kidneys under the spine at the mid part of the abdomen. They are connected to the horns of the uterus by fallopian tubes. The horns of the uterus come together in the body of the uterus, behind which is the cervix (the narrowing), which leads to the vagina and opens into the vulva under the tail.

during a season, sometimes during mating, but often for no obvious reason. At the end of the season the cervix closes and infection may build up gradually over several weeks, so that the uterus, in effect, becomes a sac of pus in the abdomen. At the point where bacteria and toxins start to escape into the blood, affected female dogs become generally unwell and may show signs of non-specific illness or even circulatory collapse. They can even die as a consequence of overwhelming infection and septicemia.

Male reproductive system

In the male, each testicle in the scrotum is connected by the vas deferens via the prostate and several other smaller glands in the pelvic area to the urethra in the penis.

What is
Neutering

In neutered (spayed) female dogs, the ovaries and part of the uterus are removed so that reproductive hormone levels do not fluctuate and estrus does not occur. In neutered (castrated) males, removing the testicles reduces male hormone levels and prevents sperm production, so that neutered males rarely have the inclination to mate and are sterile.

Symptoms

- The presence of a purulent (pus-containing) or bloody vaginal discharge. Initially, owners sometimes mistake this for a seasonal discharge, but it is usually heavier, lasts longer, and can be malodorous. In some cases, the cervix remains closed when pyometra occurs and the dog shows no vaginal discharge. These cases can be harder to diagnose.
- Increased drinking, loss of appetite, vomiting. Although these are all signs of general ill-health, in an unneutered female dog they are sufficiently suggestive of pyometra to warrant further investigation to rule out this condition.

Diagnosis In most cases, the presence of a purulent vaginal discharge is sufficient for diagnosis. X-rays or ultrasound scanning may show enlargement of the uterus with fluid within. Blood tests may show raised white blood cell levels, indicating a source of infection.

Treatment Pyometra is extremely unlikely to respond to normal medical therapy, as antibiotics alone cannot penetrate the pus in the affected dog's uterus and so cannot resolve the infection. Instead, the infection must be removed, which usually necessitates emergency surgical treatment to perform an ovariohysterectomy. Affected dogs also need antibiotics and anti-inflammatory

Below: *Female dogs will not tolerate mating unless they are in season and likely to be fertile. Therefore, resulting conception rates are high.*

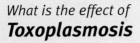

? What is the effect of
Toxoplasmosis

In dogs, toxoplasmosis (a zoonotic infection) causes symptoms ranging from low-grade malaise with no specific problems to liver disease, neurological problems, and the birth of dead or weak puppies. It can be caught from eating undercooked meat or feces from infected cats, or from contact with infected sheep. Appropriate antibiotics can be used on affected adults, but puppies are unlikely to survive.

medicines. Pain relief is needed, as both the condition and surgical ovariohysterectomy are painful. Female dogs also benefit from intravenous fluid therapy to prevent dehydration and shock until they are feeling better and no longer at risk of septicemia or circulatory shock.

UNWANTED MATING

Mismating (misalliance) does not, or course, constitute a disease. However, the risk to the female dog that can be caused by a pregnancy – and the prospect of trying to find homes for unwanted puppies when there are already so many around – may mean that owners wish to avoid their female dog conceiving and delivering a litter. In some countries, medicines are available

that can be given after mating to prevent conception, but these can result in pyometra. In the event of a misalliance, seek prompt veterinary attention to discuss the options available. Of course, spaying of female dogs not intended for breeding is far preferable.

OVARIAN AND UTERINE TUMORS

These are rare conditions.

Symptoms

- Vague symptoms include loss of appetite, abdominal pain and sometimes abdominal swelling, vomiting, weakness, and malaise.

Diagnosis X-rays and ultrasound scanning can allow tumors to be identified.

Treatment Surgical removal of masses may be curative in those female dogs where the tumor has not already spread.

MAMMARY TUMORS

These are much more common, with a high proportion of unneutered female dogs developing mammary tumors (breast cancer) later in life. With each of her seasons, the risk increases of a female dog developing mammary tumors due to the hormone surge involved. Early spaying can be preventative.

Symptoms

- While stroking, grooming, or checking over their pet, the vigilant owner usually notices lumps that develop in the mammary tissue.
- Lumps may appear close to the nipples or in the tissue between, and they may occur in

mammary tissue. This stretches from the axilla (armpit under the front leg) back to the groin area on the underside of the dog.

- Dogs do not normally show any signs of pain associated with such lumps and usually seem unaware of their presence.

Diagnosis To assess what the best treatment is likely to be, it is necessary to diagnose what type of lump is present. Lumps vary from cysts and abscesses to benign or malignant tumors, some of which may already have spread to other parts of the body, such as the lungs. In most cases, surgically removing the mass is the best initial option, although biopsy of large masses may be a good first step. While the dog is anesthetised, it is usually advisable to X-ray the chest to check that metastasis (spread of cancer) has not already occurred. Tissue samples may also be taken from nearby lymph nodes to check for cancer spread. The tissue retrieved from the mass itself can then be sent off for microscopic analysis to determine the cell type present. This yields information about the likely course of disease and thus allows the veterinarian to determine the most effective treatment.

Treatment Options include removing a more extensive area of mammary tissue or even a unilateral or bilateral mammary strip (removing all the mammary tissue on one or both sides of the dog). Spaying may help prevent the development of future, hormone-associated tumors. Radiotherapy or chemotherapy may be options in some cases.

Many dogs with mammary lumps respond well to prompt and thorough treatment. However, some types of mammary cancer can be impossible to treat effectively. In some cases,

? What is the effect of
Herpes virus

Herpes virus infection causes few symptoms in non-pregnant animals, although there may be mild respiratory disease (generally evident as a cough). Genital lesions (swollen painful genitals) are also seen in some cases. Many animals come into contact with the virus and develop an immunity. However, female dogs that meet the virus for the first time when pregnant, or that have met it before but developed a latent infection rather than become immune, may lose puppies or give birth to small, weak puppies that fade and die.

Right: *Lumps in the mammary tissue may indicate tumors or infection.*

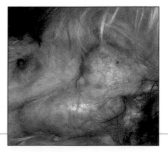

masses ulcerate (open and leak) and become so painful that the female dog's quality of life deteriorates until euthanasia becomes advisable. Affected dogs may also succumb to secondary masses elsewhere in the body.

MASTITIS

Infection in the mammary tissue can initially cause the development of a mammary lump, which owners may fear relates to a tumor. However, mastitis generally occurs in dogs that are lactating because they have just had puppies or have been in season.

Symptoms

- Mastitis causes swellings that are usually hot, hard, painful, and ill-defined.
- Affected dogs may also be unwell, with a high temperature and other associated symptoms, such as vomiting and dehydration.
- Infected mammary tissue can also rupture and leak pus and infected tissue, or pus may leak from the nipples.

Diagnosis of the type of infection present involves culturing pus samples and identifying the bacteria under laboratory conditions.

Treatment Surgical treatment may be necessary. In most cases antibiotics and anti-inflammatory pain-relieving medicines resolve the infection.

FALSE PREGNANCY

This condition follows estrus in many female dogs. It is associated with normal hormonal activity in dogs, where puppy feeding is shared

Above: *While experiencing a false pregnancy, female dogs may appear depressed and withdrawn and may exhibit "nesting" behavior, spending time in their bed with their toys.*

between pack female dogs in the wild. The situation is normally seen a few weeks after estrus and may last for three or four weeks before it spontaneously resolves.

Symptoms

- The development of mammary swelling and milk production.
- Behavioral changes, such as nesting.
- Mastitis can also occur.

Treatment is not normally necessary, although hormonal medicines may be used. Female dogs that develop mastitis may need antibiotics and anti-inflammatory medicines.

VAGINITIS

Infection or inflammation in the vagina may occur for a number of reasons. Young female dogs before their first season often have a mild vaginitis as they mature.

Symptoms

• Mucus or purulent vaginal discharge.

Diagnosis involves identifying the bacteria present on a swab.

Treatment may not be required, although some cases benefit from antibiotic treatment.

In older female dogs, vaginal discharge may indicate pregnancy loss (miscarriage/abortion) or vaginitis due to infection in the vagina, but as vaginal discharge more often relates to **pyometra**, prompt and intensive treatment may be required.

Above: *A healthy female dog mated at her most fertile time has the best chance of delivering and rearing healthy puppies.*

INFERTILITY AND PREGNANCY LOSS

In most cases, a mating that takes place when a female dog is receptive and at the appropriate stage of her estrus cycle results in pregnancy. A number of problems may cause female dogs intended for breeding not to become pregnant or to lose their pregnancy.

If a female is having difficulty becoming pregnant, it is important to ensure that mating takes place at the right time for that individual animal. Blood samples or vaginal swabs taken during estrus can make it possible to determine the best timing for mating, which varies from one female dog to another. This may improve the likelihood of conception. Prior to pregnancy, it may also be necessary to check the female for

? What is the effect of *Brucella canis*

Brucella canis, prevalent in the southern U.S., can also cause loss of pregnancy or the birth of dead or weak puppies. Infections can spread through kennels and are almost impossible to treat, although disinfection and good hygiene may prevent infection. Affected dogs may have to be removed from a breeding program. The infection is zoonotic.

bacterial or viral infections with a vaginal swab or blood tests. In addition, it may be necessary to check that the male dog's sperm is viable and to ensure that he is not passing on an infection.

Symptoms

• Loss of pregnancy in the early stages may not involve any external signs of disease or pregnancy loss. It may simply appear as though the female dog has not conceived, or she may give birth to a smaller litter or to weak or unviable puppies.

• If more advanced pregnancies are lost, the female dog is more likely to show signs of malaise and may pass tissues and fetuses.

Pregnancies can be lost due to infection. Any infection or disease that makes a female dog ill may cause her to lose her pregnancy. Injuries, malnutrition, and hormonal disorders can cause

Below: Healthy puppies are strong and motivated to suckle. Feeding the mother puppy food before and after birth will supply the nutrients she needs.

infertility, and some otherwise healthy female dogs simply do not make viable eggs and thus cannot conceive.

Male reproductive diseases

As in females, disease associated with the reproductive organs can occur in unneutered males, but most are prevented or treated by neutering. Reproductive disease in young males is fairly uncommon; problems most often crop up in older males.

UNDESCENDED TESTICLES (CRYPTORCHIDISM)

The testicles are formed in the abdomen just behind the kidneys, but gradually move down,

Below: An empty scrotum in an entire male indicates cryptorchidism, a condition in which the testicles do not descend from the abdomen.

passing through an opening in the groin to come to lie under the skin in the scrotum. This maintains them at a lower temperature than if they were in the abdomen, which is essential for their normal function.

From a few weeks of age, most male puppies have two descended testicles located in the scrotum. If they are not present in the scrotum by the time the puppy is six to nine months old, they are unlikely to descend and may remain located in the abdomen. This is significant, because a relatively high proportion of undescended testicles develop tumors, even in young dogs.

Symptoms

• One or both testicles do not descend.

Treatment It is particularly important for affected dogs to be castrated, even though removing abdominal testicles is trickier than normal castration.

TESTICULAR TUMORS OR MASSES

Symptoms

• Old dogs sometimes develop lumps in the testicles, as do younger, cryptorchid dogs.

Treatment Most lumps are benign and respond well to surgical removal by castration. However, some can spread to nearby tissues or to other organs and may need further treatment.

PROSTATIC HYPERPLASIA / CYST / TUMOR

Several diseases can occur in the prostate and can cause fairly similar symptoms.

Left: *Prolonged straining can indicate prostatic disease. Treatment for most causes of this condition can be effective.*

Symptoms

- Prostatic swelling, which can partially block the urethra. This makes it harder for the dog to pass a strong stream of urine and empty his bladder properly, so that he strains to urinate.
- Urinary discoloration (e.g., bloody or darkened urine) may be evident, so that symptoms sometimes appear similar to those of **cystitis**.
- The rectum may also be narrowed by prostatic swelling, causing constipation.

Diagnosis Examination may include blood and urine tests and laboratory examination of samples retrieved from the prostate via a catheter. X-rays and ultrasound scans of the area may also be needed.

Treatment Dogs with prostatic infections often need long courses of antibiotics. Those with hormone-related prostatic hyperplasia (swelling) benefit from castration, as do those with prostatic tumors, since many are hormone related. Cysts and tumors in the prostate may also necessitate surgical treatment.

Most prostatic diseases are treatable and castration can prevent their recurrence. However, some prostatic tumors may be impossible to treat effectively.

ANAL ADENOMAS / CARCINOMAS

Tumors may form in the perineum (the region of skin around the anus). These may also relate to levels of male hormones in unneutered males.

Symptoms

- Although these masses do not normally spread elsewhere, they can affect a dog's ability to defecate normally and may require removal.

Treatment Many masses are slow-growing and may not need removing, but castration may be recommended to reduce their speed of growth.

Hormonal problems

Because of the wide range of effects of the hormones, the symptoms experienced by dogs with hormonal, or endocrine, diseases are extremely variable.

Symptoms

- Increased drinking and urination.
- Decreased or increased eating.
- Breathlessness, lethargy.
- Weight loss or weight gain.
- Vomiting and diarrhea.
- Hair loss, usually symmetrical in the flank area, with no concurrent itchiness.

Diagnosis

- Normal blood screen tests provide information regarding the levels of blood cells and various enzymes and chemicals in the body that relate to liver and kidney function and the status of other organs. These levels may vary with specific hormonal problems.
- Specific blood tests reveal the levels of the different hormones and relevant chemicals.
- Ultrasound scanning or MRI can be particularly useful, as they allow detailed images of soft tissues to be examined.

Treatments

- Appropriate medicines to supplement or reduce hormone levels.

- In some cases, surgical treatments may be helpful.

Growth hormone disorders

Growth hormone is produced by the pituitary gland at the base of the brain after stimulation from the hypothalamus.

?

What does it do
The hormonal system

The hormonal system consists of a network of glands that each produce chemicals called hormones. These are released into the blood and have wide-ranging effects. Hormones control many of the most fundamental body processes, from the rate of metabolism (the speed at which the reactions in the body take place and the heart beats) to the animal's ability to respond to stress to the regulation of blood sugar levels. Hormones also control growth, development, and sexual behavior. They affect all the organs in the body and are also involved in mood and emotions.

THE HORMONAL SYSTEM

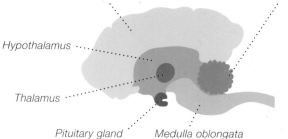

Cerebral hemispheres

Cerebellum

Hypothalamus

Thalamus

Pituitary gland

Medulla oblongata

In the brain, an area called the hypothalamus controls the function of the pituitary gland, also in the brain.

The thyroid gland in the neck controls the speed of metabolism.

The parathyroid gland located beside it is involved in regulating calcium levels in the body.

The adrenal glands next to the kidneys help regulate electrolyte balance within the body and control the body's response to stress.

The ovaries and testicles produce sex hormones that control reproductive behavior.

The pituitary gland secretes hormones into the bloodstream that regulate the activity of other glands in the body. It also secretes growth hormone, which controls growth and development, and anti-diuretic hormone, which controls the kidney's ability to conserve water.

Insulin produced by the pancreas controls blood sugar levels.

LACK OF PRODUCTION OF GROWTH HORMONE

A rare condition in some puppies (most often German Shepherds) involves a lack of production of growth hormone.

Symptoms

- Puppies fail to grow normally and do not grow an adult hair coat. Areas of hair loss may be seen, and skin disorders are common.
- Puppies' teeth may not erupt normally, and the growth plates in the bones do not close normally.
- Puppies remain small and tend to be nervous and slow to learn.

Diagnosis Blood tests can confirm lack of growth hormone.

Treatment with growth hormone is possible, but even with treatment these puppies have a short life expectancy.

EXCESSIVE PRODUCTION OF GROWTH HORMONE

Elderly dogs – mostly unneutered females – may produce excessive amounts of growth hormone or growth hormone-like chemicals, causing overgrowth of bone and cartilage (acromegaly).

Symptoms

- Thickening and growth of the head, limbs, and paws. The skin may also become thickened.
- Increased appetite and thirst (possibly).
- Breathlessness (possibly).
- **Diabetes mellitus** may develop as the tissues in the body become resistant to the effects of insulin.
- Heart disease may occur.

Diagnosis This condition may be difficult to diagnose, but blood tests can be helpful.

Treatment Spaying may resolve many of the symptoms. Other treatments may be necessary.

Left: Dogs with hormonal disease are often lethargic. This is one of many possible symptoms that need investigation.

Hypothyroidism

Reduced production of thyroid hormones from the thyroid gland in the neck can follow inflammatory disease in this gland, cancer of the thyroid gland, or a failure of normal thyroid control by the pituitary and hypothalamus. Wide-ranging symptoms occur, relating to the various functions of thyroid hormones in controlling the rate of metabolism and organ activity throughout the body.

Symptoms

- Lethargy and malaise.
- Weight gain.
- Changes in reproductive behavior and reduced fertility (in unneutered dogs).
- Greasiness of the coat, hair loss (often symmetrical on the flanks), and coat color changes.
- Affected dogs feel cold and often choose to lie right next to the fire.
- Thyroid disease may also be associated with **megaesophagus** and **laryngeal paralysis**, and may be detected when dogs show evidence of a low heart rate or **heart disease**.
- Eye problems, such as ulceration or changes in the cornea (surface of the eye), are also common.
- Some affected dogs will also suffer intestinal problems, such as constipation or diarrhea.

Diagnosis This combination of symptoms may give a suspicion of hypothyroidism, but blood tests are needed to make a diagnosis. A blood screen may show mild anemia and some other

Above: *German Shepherd Dog puppies occasionally suffer from lack of growth hormone. Blood tests can confirm the condition.*

subtle signs consistent with thyroid disease. Specific hormone tests generally show low levels of circulating thyroid hormones and high levels of the hormones that normally trigger their release (but cannot because the thyroid is not working). Tests can also be done to demonstrate an inadequate response of the thyroid gland to injected thyroid-stimulating hormone.

Many dogs with other chronic diseases develop low thyroid levels and thyroid disease, so in some cases there may also be a further underlying problem that needs to be resolved.

Treatment consists of giving dogs thyroid replacement therapy, which can result in rapid resolution of their symptoms. Individual dogs vary as to the dose they need, so blood tests are taken to monitor thyroid hormone levels, allowing the dose of medication to be adjusted accordingly. Initially, tests may be needed after four weeks; in the long term, checks every six months may be required.

Parathyroid disorders

The parathyroid glands (next to the thyroid glands) are involved in regulating the amounts of calcium in the body. Disorders of these glands can result in abnormally high calcium levels, causing muscle and bone weakness.

Symptoms
- Muscle tremors and spasms may develop.
- Disease in other organs, such as the kidneys, due to high calcium levels.

Treatment Surgical treatment may be needed to remove diseased glands.

Medical treatment may be appropriate to supplement calcium and Vitamin D levels in dogs with reduced parathyroid function.

Adrenal gland disorders

The adrenal glands are involved in regulating electrolyte levels and various processes in the body. Disease causes a wide range of symptoms.

CUSHING'S DISEASE

Hyperadrenocorticism (Cushing's disease) involves overproduction of corticosteroid hormones (e.g., cortisol) from the adrenal glands. This

> **!**
>
> *Be aware*
> ## *Pancreatic tumors*
>
> *Dogs with pancreatic tumors sometimes produce an excess of insulin, leading to reduced blood sugar levels. Weakness and lethargy, together with abdominal pain, may be evident; affected dogs may collapse due to low blood sugar.*

can occur because of the development of a hormone-producing tumor in an adrenal gland. Alternatively, it may result from overproduction of the chemical produced by the pituitary, which stimulates the release of corticosteroids due to a tumor in the pituitary gland.

Symptoms
- Breathlessness, weakness, and lethargy.
- Abdominal swelling.
- Some dogs may also experience increased appetite and thirst, vomiting, and diarrhea.
- Skin tone may change; affected dogs often having thinned skin that heals poorly if damaged. Dark blemishes may develop, crusty calcium deposits may be seen, and patches of symmetrical hair loss are common.
- Poor immunity, so dogs become more susceptible to disease.
- Muscle wastage is also common. Affected dogs generally develop a potbellied, thin-backed appearance.

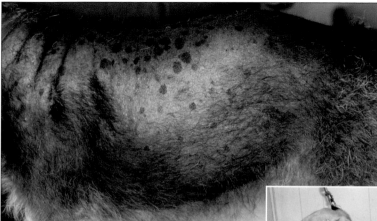

Left: *Hair loss and skin discoloration in a dog with Cushing's disease.*

Below: *Hormonal conditions can cause weight loss and neurological problems, such as hind limb weakness.*

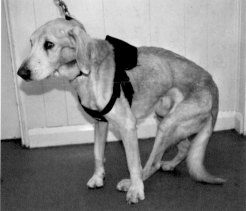

• Hyperadrenocorticism also predisposes dogs to developing **diabetes mellitus**, so affected dogs may also need treatment for this.

The same symptoms of disease may also occur in dogs treated with corticosteroids to treat other conditions, particularly if they are given high doses for a long time.

Diagnosis of this condition can be difficult because its effects in the body are variable. Blood tests may show raised white blood cell levels and raised levels of certain liver enzymes, but these and other changes are not always consistent. Further tests can assay cortisol levels, although these vary enormously through the day and so are not, on their own, diagnostic. The most helpful tests are those that measure cortisol levels before and after injections of the hormone that stimulates or suppresses their release, thereby demonstrating the excessive and uncontrolled activity of the pituitary/adrenal glands.

Treatment involves reducing the levels of circulating steroids by suppressing their release from the adrenal gland. Several medicines exist that work in different ways and may suit different dogs. Surgical removal of the affected adrenal gland or radiation therapy are also appropriate in some cases. Dogs receiving medical treatment need ongoing monitoring of their blood every few weeks/months, and levels of medication may need to be adjusted according to their response.

Although the disease is not curable, many dogs do well on ongoing therapy for hyperadrenocorticism.

ADDISON'S DISEASE

Hypoadrenocorticism (Addison's disease) involves the underproduction of steroid hormones by the adrenal gland. It occurs if the adrenal glands become damaged or diseased for a number of reasons. Symptoms can also follow the sudden withdrawal of steroid medication. In addition to producing the corticosteroids needed to enable an animal to cope with stress and change in its life, the adrenal glands also make mineralocortacoids. These control the body's ability to conserve salts in the diet, which are needed to maintain muscle and heart activity.

Hypoadrenocorticism usually causes waxing and waning symptoms of vague ill health that develop over a period of time. Symptoms are worse at times of stress, such as after staying in a different house, mixing with other dogs, going out somewhere unusual, or having an unusually high level of exercise.

Symptoms

• Weakness and collapse.

• Vomiting and sometimes diarrhea.

• During an episode, dogs may also have a low heart rate and experience abdominal pain.

! *Be aware*

Collapse/coma

Although the onset of thyroid disease, Addison's disease, and diabetes mellitus are normally gradual processes, they can occasionally cause collapse/coma, requiring emergency and intensive treatment.

Diagnosis of this condition can be difficult, as affected dogs vary, but specific changes in blood electrolyte (salt) levels are common. Blood tests that measure the adrenal gland's response to stimulatory chemicals are usually diagnostic. **Treatment** involves giving a daily dose of steroid medication and a medicine that enables the dog to conserve salts in the body. Dietary salt may also need to be supplemented initially. Affected dogs usually respond very well to treatment.

Diabetes

Diabetes is a hormonal disorder that causes a marked increase in drinking and urination.

DIABETES MELLITUS (SUGAR DIABETES)

After a meal, rising blood glucose (sugar) levels should cause the release of insulin from the pancreas, enabling sugar to be stored in the liver. This glucose can then be released into the blood when the dog is hungry and has low blood sugar levels. Failure of the pancreas to release insulin, or of the body to respond to insulin (which can occur in obese animals), can result in uncontrolled glucose levels in the blood. When glucose levels get too high, glucose can leak into the urine, sucking water with it. Sugars can also leak into the brain and into the lenses in the eyes.

Symptoms

- Weakness, lethargy, and depression or even coma, due to fluctuating sugar levels.
- Increased urination and increased thirst.
- Crystalline cataracts in the eyes due to sugar deposits.
- Muscle wastage.
- Neurological problems, such as limb weakness and loss of normal sensation.
- Skin disease.

Below: *Sugar deposits in the lenses of the eyes can cause whitish opaque cataracts to develop.*

- Ketoacidosis (a circulatory disorder) can result if sugar levels fluctuate severely, which can lead to coma and death.

Diagnosis entails checking blood glucose levels, often at two-hour intervals over a twenty-four-hour period, to assess the body's response to sugars in the diet. Insulin levels can also be measured.

Treatment generally involves feeding special food that gives a more gradual release of sugar than normal food, together with insulin therapy (as once- or twice-daily injections) to enable dogs to store the sugar released. Surgical treatment involving gene therapy may soon be available.

DIABETES INSIPIDIS

Like diabetes mellitus, diabetes insipidis is characterised by an increase in drinking and urination. However, this rarer disease relates to failure of production of antidiuretic hormone (ADH) by the pituitary gland, which is needed to enable the kidneys to conserve water.

Symptoms

- Affected dogs drink excessively and pass increased amounts of very dilute urine.
- Weight loss and weakness can also result.

Diagnosis involves depriving the dog of water under controlled conditions and measuring the concentration of the urine to establish that the dog is unable to create more concentrated urine.

Treatment Synthetic ADH can be given to enable the dog to conserve water and make more concentrated urine.

Circulatory/blood and lymph disorders

Disorders in the circulatory system can result in a number of symptoms.

Symptoms

- Breathlessness and weakness due to low levels of oxygen in the blood or reduced red blood cell levels.
- Bruising may be seen if insufficient platelet numbers are present.
- Blood may also be lost into the lungs and bowel, which can cause coughing of blood and darkening of the feces respectively.
- Other symptoms can develop, as circulatory disorders affect all parts of the body. Increased drinking, decreased appetite, and lethargy and weakness are common.

Diagnosis

- Blood tests to measure red and white blood cell and platelet levels.
- Tests showing levels of enzymes and other chemicals relating to liver, kidney, bone, and heart function are also useful.
- A blood smear can be examined under a microscope to assess blood cell shape and structure, as well as to count absolute numbers of cells. Parasites in the blood may be detectable.
- Specific tests indicating **immune-mediated diseases**, **lymphoma**, and the presence of antibodies to specific **blood parasites** are also helpful.

Treatments

Specific treatments include

- Antiparasitic medicines to treat blood parasites.
- Medicines that modulate the activity of the immune system to treat immune-mediated disease.

? What does it do
The blood

Blood is made up of red blood cells, white blood cells, platelets, and plasma, which itself consists of water, proteins, products of digestion, hormones, antibodies, and other chemicals. Red and white blood cells and platelets are made in the bone marrow. Red cells, needed for carrying oxygen, mature in the spleen and are stored there until needed.

White blood cells, involved in fighting disease, are released into the bloodstream and lymph nodes.

Platelets, together with chemicals called clotting factors, allow the blood to clot if an injury occurs.

THE BLOOD CIRCULATION SYSTEM

The heart pumps blood around the body, carrying vital nutrients, oxygen, and immune cells to the periphery, as well as carrying waste products for excretion.

The heart is located in a protected position within the chest.

Fluid also travels away from the tissues and gastrointestinal tract in lymphatics. These drain back into the bloodstream via lymph nodes, where immune cells are located that can recognize and respond to signs of infection coming from the tissues.

Blood is pumped by the heart through the lungs to pick up oxygen.

It is then pumped again into arteries and then smaller and smaller arterioles and capillaries to reach all parts of the body, bringing nutrients and oxygen.

Waste products in the body diffuse into veins and are carried back to the heart and eventually to the liver and kidneys for detoxification and excretion.

? What are
Steroids

Steroids, or corticosteroids, are medicines that are very strongly anti-inflammatory. They can be used to treat allergic conditions involving the skin, bowel, or lungs, and are also used to treat immune-mediated diseases and some cancers.

- Supportive treatments, such as intravenous fluids and even blood transfusions, may also be needed.
- Other therapies that may be appropriate include chemotherapy and surgical treatment for lymphoma. Medicines may also be needed to support other organ systems in the body compromised by poor circulation.

Anemia

Insufficient levels of circulating red blood cells – anemia – may occur for a number of reasons. **Kidney disease** can result in anemia due to reduced production of erythropoetin by the kidneys. (This hormone normally promotes red blood cell production.) Malnutrition or chronic disease of any kind can result in anemia. Other specific conditions include **immune-mediated hemolytic anemia**, which occurs when the body makes antibodies that destroy its own red blood cells. Anemia may be due to blood loss following an injury, internal bleeding (e.g., from a splenic tumor), or poisoning with rodenticides. Another potential cause of anemia is paracetamol/acetaminophen poisoning. This can arise either as a result of the dog having accidental access to these drugs or because an owner seeks to relieve his or her dog's pain without understanding that paracetamol/acetaminophen can be toxic for dogs. These drugs can also cause liver and kidney disease.

Symptoms

- Weakness and breathlessness due to reduced oxygenation of the blood and the tissues of the body.
- Heart and pulse rates are elevated as the body tries to compensate for reduced oxygen levels by pumping blood faster.
- Mucous membranes, such as the gums, tend to be pale.
- Anemia that follows disease in other organs tends to cause a gradual onset of mild symptoms such as lethargy and malaise.
- Sudden onset causes of anemia, such as acute conditions and blood loss, cause dramatic symptoms such as weakness, labored breathing, and collapse. These require emergency treatment.

Treatment There are various ways of treating the causes of anemia, such as surgical removal of splenic tumors or using rodenticide antidotes. Specific life-saving measures also include putting the affected animal on an intravenous drip to protect blood pressure and circulation.

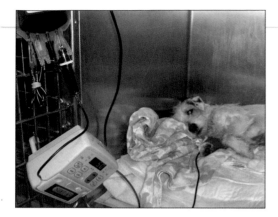

Above: *A potentially life-saving blood transfusion can be used to replace a deficit in red blood cells.*

In some cases, a blood transfusion may also be necessary.

IMMUNE-MEDIATED HEMOLYTIC ANEMIA

This is a sudden onset disease that may follow a known stressful event, infection, or estrus. It may also be linked with the use of certain medicines and can be seen in dogs with cancer.

Symptoms
• Breathlessness and weakness.

Diagnosis Blood tests reveal low red blood cell numbers, as well as raised liver enzymes and bilirubin levels. (These relate to the increased workload of the liver in recycling hemoglobin.) Specific tests can be carried out to try to identify the presence of abnormal antibodies that cause the problem.

Treatment generally involves medicines that suppress the immune system and thus reduce the activity of the auto-antibodies. Such medicines include corticosteroids and other cytotoxic medicines.

Depending on the cause of the condition, some dogs respond well to treatment and eventually can be weaned off medication, whereas others are hard to control and need ongoing treatment if they are to have a chance of survival.

SPLENIC TUMORS

The role of the spleen is to store red blood cells prior to release into the bloodstream. This means that disease in the spleen can cause

? *What is* **Blood transfusion**

Blood can be taken from a donor dog and transfused into a recipient. Blood may be taken from a healthy donor or purchased from a canine blood bank. Although most dogs do not have naturally occurring antibodies that cause transfusion reactions, it is advisable to cross-match blood before transfusion to avoid an adverse reaction. Dogs that have had previous transfusions may have developed antibodies against donor blood, so it is particularly important to test such candidates to ensure that an adverse reaction will not occur.

anemia due to lack of release of red blood cells into the circulation, or hemorrhage from the spleen. Splenic tumors are relatively common, particularly in older dogs.

Symptoms
- Lethargy, breathlessness.
- Pale mucous membranes.
- Sometimes an abdominal mass in the spleen is palpable.

Diagnosis includes blood tests that indicate anemia, and abdominal X-rays. If left undiagnosed, tumors may start to bleed into the abdomen, causing sudden blood loss and collapse.

Treatment Surgically removing the spleen can be curative; dogs can live a relatively normal life without a spleen. However, in some cases, tumors spread to other organs in the abdomen, and removing all of them may not be possible.

RAT POISONING
Anticoagulant rodenticides are commonly used to kill rats and mice, but sadly both the poison itself and the dead rodents are palatable and dangerous to dogs. These poisons work by blocking vitamin K production, which is needed to allow normal blood clotting. Signs of toxicity can take several days to develop as the body's stores of vitamin K are used up. Once symptoms have started to develop, death can follow quickly without emergency measures.

Symptoms
- Severe internal hemorrhage, with bleeding into the bowel.
- Bloodstained vomit and diarrhea may be evident.
- Bruising under the skin.
- Blood may be lost into the bladder (causing urinary discoloration), the joints (causing

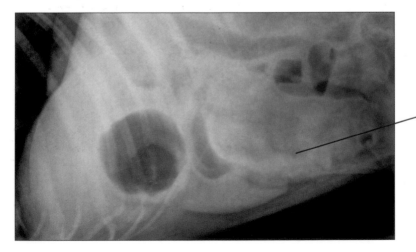

The large mass in this dog's abdomen is a splenic tumor that was surgically removed.

Right: Gum color can be an important indicator of the healthiness of the circulation. Anemic dogs or those with circulatory disorders may have pale gums and poor circulation.

lameness), the brain (causing seizures), and the respiratory system (causing nose bleeds and coughing of blood).

Treatment includes intravenous fluid therapy, blood transfusions, and supportive medication. Vitamin K therapy can take one to two days to stop hemorrhage occurring, as clotting factors have to be synthesized. Once severe symptoms develop, treatment may not be effective.

Infectious circulatory diseases

Some circulatory diseases result from infection with organisms that destroy blood cells.

BABESIOSIS

The tick-borne disease babesiosis, caused by the protozoan parasite *Babesia*, is found in much of southern Europe, parts of the U.S., and many other areas with a warm climate. Puppies can develop the disease in the womb, having been infected through the placenta, and blood transfusions can also be a source of infection. However, dogs are normally infected by the bite of a carrier tick. This injects the *Babesia* parasite into the circulation, where the organisms multiply in the red blood cells, causing damage so that anemia results. Symptoms normally take two to three weeks to develop. If untreated, most dogs die within days, although some dogs have sufficient resistance to live, albeit still showing signs of disease.

Symptoms
- Fever, lethargy, and malaise.
- Breathlessness, pale mucous membranes, and increased heart rate typical of anemia.

Diagnosis Blood tests confirm anemia, but a specific diagnosis of babesiosis can usually be made after microscope examination of a blood smear reveals *Babesia* parasites within infected red blood cells. Blood tests are also available that confirm the presence of *Babesia* antibodies in infected dogs.

Treatment If diagnosed early enough, babesiosis can be treated with specific medication. However, it can also be prevented by treating dogs with anti-tick parasiticides before they go into endemic areas.

EHRLICHIOSIS

This tends to occur mostly in dogs living in warm temperate or tropical regions, where the ticks that carry it are common. *Ehrlichia* bacteria multiply in cells in the blood, resulting in damage to these cells and low platelet and blood cell numbers.

Dogs that live in endemic areas have some natural resistance and may be infected for years but show only mild symptoms. Dogs imported from other areas or traveling through endemic areas are extremely susceptible and suffer severe disease that can prove fatal within days to weeks.

Symptoms
- Lethargy and weakness.
- Fever and swelling of the spleen.

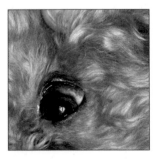

Left: *A bleed into the white of the eye can occur due to injury or as a result of a clotting disorder due to circulatory or liver disease.*

- Hemorrhages due to low platelet numbers, resulting in nose bleeds, as well as lameness and neurological symptoms such as seizures.
- Eye disease may also result.

Diagnosis involves blood tests and laboratory examination of a blood smear.

Treatment with medicines effective against *Ehrlichia* can be curative if started sufficiently soon after infection.

Lymphoma/leukemia

Lymphoma is one of the most common types of neoplastic (cancerous) disease in dogs. It occurs when white blood cells become cancerous in soft tissues such as the lymph nodes, skin, spleen, liver, bowel wall, and other organs, causing masses to develop in these tissues. Closely related, leukemia refers to neoplasia of these types of cells in the bone marrow and the blood.

Symptoms
- Lethargy and weakness (both lymphoma and leukemia).
- Lymphoma can also cause coughing and breathlessness, increased drinking, vomiting, and diarrhea, and even skin lumps, depending on which tissues are affected.
- Swelling of the lymph nodes and other organs may also be evident.
- Loss of appetite and weight loss may occur.
- Affected dogs may become increasingly susceptible to infection, and resultant bleeding disorders may lead to hemorrhage, joint pain, and neurological signs.

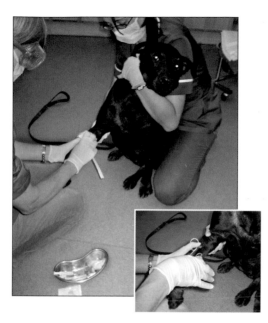

or infusions (given in a drip) at variable intervals. Ongoing treatment and monitoring is necessary, and outcomes vary depending on the exact type of neoplasia present. Despite treatment, some dogs die within days to weeks, but with appropriate treatment others live and are happy for months to years.

Chemotherapy medications – sometimes following surgery to remove or reduce any large masses – can be effective, often with few side effects. Palliative treatment (pain relief and supportive care until the quality of life diminishes and becomes untenable) may be offered for those dogs that are not good candidates for chemotherapy.

Above: Chemotherapy can be very effective in the treatment of lymphoma. Here, a Rottweiler is receiving an infusion directly into the bloodstream.

Diagnosis may be possible following blood tests and examination of a blood smear to detect abnormal cells. However, chest and abdominal X-rays and ultrasound scans may be needed to reveal masses in the internal organs. Tissue aspirates or biopsies may be needed to allow diagnosis. Specific blood tests for lymphoma are also available.

Treatment Various regimens exist, depending on the exact type of cancer present. However, most include daily tablets, as well as injections

Below:
Chemotherapy regimens can allow dogs to enjoy a good quality of life.

Heart disease

Heart diseases are relatively common, particularly in older dogs that may suffer from inadequate heart function. Dogs with heart disease generally suffer symptoms that relate to lack of nutrient and oxygen supply to their tissues, but they rarely experience sudden collapsing episodes. Because blockage of the blood vessels in the heart wall does not normally happen, dogs do not usually experience painful "heart attacks."

Symptoms

- Lethargy and weakness.
- Coughing, breathlessness, and retching if fluid builds up in the lungs due to poor heart function. (This is known as congestive heart failure, CHF.)
- Many dogs with heart disease lose weight due to loss of appetite and difficulty eating when they are breathless.

Diagnosis

- Clinical examination and auscultation (listening with a stethoscope) of affected dogs may allow a veterinarian to recognize a heart problem. However, further investigation is usually needed to diagnose the type of disease present so that appropriate treatment can be chosen.
- Echocardiography (ultrasound scanning of the heart) allows the heart to be imaged, revealing leaky or narrowed heart valves.
- Electrocardiography (an ECG) assesses the electrical activity of the heart and can identify heart rhythm disturbances.
- X-rays of the chest can also be helpful in some cases, as it may reveal changes in the size, shape, or contour of the heart. It can also show secondary changes in the lungs.

Treatments

- Medicines that enable the heart to beat more effectively or that aid circulation of the blood.
- Diuretics can shift excess fluid out of the circulation and ease the workload of the heart.
- Medication may also be prescribed to change the heart rate or rhythm.
- Dogs with heartworm disease benefit from antiparasitic medicines.
- Pacemaker surgery may be appropriate in some dogs with rhythm disturbances.

Murmurs/valvular leakage

The most common types of heart problem relate to disease in the valves of the heart, which often occurs with age. Many dogs develop leaky heart valves as they get older, with the result that with each beat, some blood is forced backward rather than out into the circulation. The result is a reduction in the circulation of blood and a buildup of fluid in the lungs and other organs, such as the liver. Murmurs may also occur in dogs of varying age with narrowed valves or vessels, with a similar effect on heart blood flow.

HOW THE HEART WORKS

Located in the middle of the chest, the heart is a muscular pump divided into two sides, allowing blood to travel in two separate systems.

From the right ventricle, blood passes to the lungs, where it picks up oxygen.

Oxygenated blood returns to the left side of the heart.

Blood returns to the right side of the heart in the veins, which empty it into the right atrium.

The pumping of the heart is controlled by the pacemaker, an area in the atria wall from which nerve impulses spread across the heart in a regular manner, resulting in contractions that pump blood.

From here, it passes through the main atrioventricular valve to the right ventricle.

Blood is pumped from the left ventricle of the heart out to the tissues and organs of the body, carrying oxygen and nutrients.

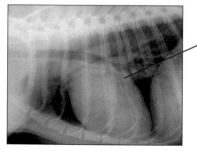

The normal heart is silhouetted clearly against the lungs.

Heart enlargement and fluid retention in the lungs reduces the clarity on this chest X-ray.

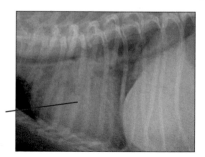

Symptoms

- To the veterinarian listening with a stethoscope, abnormal blood flow may be audible as a murmur, or abnormal heart sound, so that the normal "lub-dub, lub-dub" of the heart is superimposed with a whooshing sound of variable intensity.
- Murmurs may be picked up when apparently healthy dogs are examined or may be detected when examining a dog with symptoms consistent with congestive heart failure.

Diagnosis To determine the relevance of a murmur, further investigation with echocardiography may be necessary to assess the valves and the blood flow through the heart. Any abnormal movement of blood can be measured and its significance assessed. ECG and chest X-rays may also be helpful. An accurate assessment helps the veterinarian choose the most appropriate treatment regimen.

Treatment Medication can aid heart function for months or years before a dog's heart function deteriorates to the point where it can no longer be controlled.

Rhythm disturbances, or arrythmias

These may occur if the electrical activity of the heart is abnormal. The consequence can be a faster- or slower-than-normal heart rate, or an irregular heartbeat. If the heart is beating too fast it may not be able to fill properly between beats and, as with a slow heart, the blood circulation may be adversely affected.

Rhythm disturbances can also occur in dogs with electrolyte abnormalities due to other diseases. **Addison's disease**, gastrointestinal problems, and **burns** can all result in high potassium levels, which may cause the heart to slow down and can contribute to dangerous heart disease.

Symptoms

- Weakness and collapse may result when the circulation is inadequate.

Left: Some Cavalier King Charles Spaniels suffer from a hereditary form of valvular heart disease.

Above: Checking the pulse with a stethoscope allows the veterinarian to assess heart activity.

- Dogs may also develop signs of congestive heart disease.

Diagnosis Rhythm disturbances generally show up best on ECG.

Treatment to normalize electrolyte levels may be required, and medicines may also be needed to help speed or slow the heart rate or to aid normal electrical activity in the heart.

DILATED CARDIOMYOPATHY

This involves weakness of the muscle of the heart, resulting in enlargement of the heart.

Symptoms

- The swollen heart cannot contract effectively to pump blood, and congestive heart failure generally follows.

Diagnosis A thorough clinical examination, combined with echocardiography and, possibly, X-rays. ECG can also be helpful.

Treatment includes medicines that assist heart function. Diuretics may be needed to remove excess fluid from the body. Medicines to slow the speed of the heart may also be helpful.

Although medication helps to stabilize affected dogs, long-term survival is relatively poor.

Heartworms

Some parasitic conditions, such as heartworms, may also cause heart disease.

AMERICAN HEARTWORM

Dirofilaria immitis is widespread throughout the Americas and much of southern Europe. *Dirofilaria* is spread by infected mosquitoes. After a bite transmits *Dirofilaria*, the parasite travels through the body to the right ventricle of the heart and the pulmonary arteries in the lungs. There, it continues to mature and cause damage to the heart and blood vessels. Adult worms pass microfilariae (tiny larvae) into the blood. These circulate in the blood and are infective if eaten by a mosquito, where they develop further, before being injected back into another dog when the mosquito feeds again.

Symptoms

- No symptoms at all or signs of heart disease, such as weakness, malaise, breathlessness, and coughing. Coughed-up material may contain blood.
- Symptoms relating to **anemia**, such as weakness and pallor.

• Symptoms relating to partial blockage of the blood vessels supplying the lungs. This can result in high blood pressure, which can cause liver failure and swelling of the abdomen with fluid.

Diagnosis Blood tests can be used to detect evidence of the worms and their larvae in the blood. The degree to which secondary heart disease has progressed can be assessed using echocardiography, X-rays, and, in some cases, ECG.

Treatment of heartworm infestation is tricky, as suddenly killing large numbers of worms in the heart can cause shock, circulatory collapse, and even death. Pulmonary emboli (i.e., the blockage of blood vessels in the lungs) may also occur.

Protocols are available for heartworm treatment that try to minimize such problems. Treatment of congestive heart failure may also be necessary.

More importantly, heartworm infection should be prevented in endemic areas using medicines prophylactically. Regular monthly worming with an effective product prevents American heartworm disease. Medicines effective against heartworm infestation usually protect dogs against intestinal worms as well.

Dirofilaria is zoonotic, although it does not normally cause serious disease in humans.

EUROPEAN HEARTWORM/LUNGWORM

Although rare in the U.S., *Angiostrongylus vasorumis* is found throughout many parts of the world. This parasitic worm lives in the pulmonary artery and right ventricle of dogs, causing damage and releasing larvae that are coughed up, swallowed, and passed in feces. The larvae then pass a phase of their life cycle in slugs and snails before infecting a dog when it eats a carrier mollusc, or possibly when a dog comes into contact with infected slime from one. The larvae then travel through the body to the

HEARTWORM LIFE CYCLE

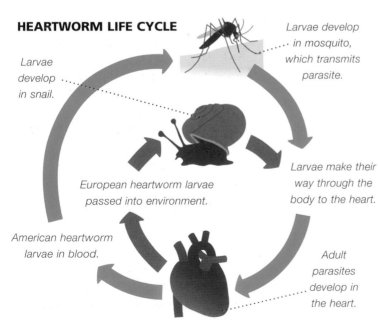

Larvae develop in mosquito, which transmits parasite.

Larvae develop in snail.

European heartworm larvae passed into environment.

Larvae make their way through the body to the heart.

American heartworm larvae in blood.

Adult parasites develop in the heart.

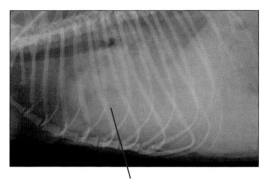

Pericardial and mediastinal disease may lead to the normal heart shadow on a chest X-ray being obscured.

heart, where they can continue their life cycle. They may cause damage to other organs such as the liver, kidney, or brain along the way.

Symptoms
- Some dogs show few symptoms, but common signs mimic those seen in dogs infested with American heartworms.
- Damage caused by larvae migrating through the body may result in neurological disease (such as **seizures** and paralysis).
- Blindness and **liver** and **kidney disease** may also be seen.
- Hemorrhage is possible.

Diagnosis The presence of these worms can be confirmed by examining fecal samples from affected dogs and finding infective larvae. Blood tests may also be helpful. Echocardiography and X-rays may be needed to assess heart function.

Treatment Affected dogs may need treatment for their heart and **circulatory disease**, as well as antiparasitic medicines to kill the worms involved. Preventative medication may also be advisable, and new products are now available that can be used monthly to help prevent *Angiostrongylus* infestation in endemic areas.

Pericardial and mediastinal disease

Infection in the pericardium (the sac that surrounds the heart) can result in pericarditis, which leads to a buildup of pus in the pericardium. This has the effect of constricting the heart and making it harder for it to beat effectively.

Symptoms
- Weakness, malaise, breathlessness, and coughing.

Similar symptoms are seen after **trauma** if a dog bleeds into the pericardium, or following any other buildup of fluid there or in the mediastinum (the tissue space that lies between the two lungs).

Diagnosis is possible when an enlarged or abnormal heart shadow is seen on an X-ray. Abnormal accumulations of fluid or tissue in these areas can be identified using ultrasound scanning.

Treatment In some cases it is possible to drain pericardial fluid, thus improving heart function, which can be sustained with appropriate antibiotic treatment and supportive measures.

Respiratory disease

Diseases of the respiratory system are not unusual and may be evident in dogs of any age that suffer injury and disease to the respiratory structures.

Symptoms

Symptoms of respiratory disease include:
- Breathlessness and coughing.
- Nasal discharge, sneezing.
- Swelling of the lymph nodes in the neck.
- Coughing and choking, retching, and vomiting.
- Dogs may also be unwell, not eating their food, lethargic, and show malaise.
- A failure to oxygenate the blood sufficiently may also result in weakness and lethargy.

Diagnosis

Diagnosis may involve the following:
- Blood tests to check that affected dogs are not anemic or otherwise unwell.
- Blood tests to check for a range of infectious diseases.
- Examining the nose and throat under anesthesia.
- X-rays of the nose, throat, and chest.
- Endoscopy of the chest cavity.
- Assessing swabs and samples taken from the

Above: *Grass seeds can cause respiratory disease if they are inhaled.*

nose, throat, and lungs. Ultrasound scanning of the chest is rarely helpful, as air interferes with image quality.

Treatments

Treatments include:
- Antibiotics to fight infections.
- Anti-inflammatory medicines and antitussives (anticough medicines) to help reduce the symptoms of respiratory problems.
- Bronchodilators may help the airways open up and allow more air to pass through.

With treatment, many causes of respiratory disease are controllable or curable.

Upper respiratory diseases

Upper respiratory diseases often cause dogs to develop sneezing and nasal discharge.

NASAL FOREIGN BODIES

Common culprits include grass seed heads and fragments of food or toys.

Symptoms

Typical signs of an acute onset problem include:
- Rubbing at the nose, sneezing.
- Nasal discharge, often containing blood.

Diagnosis A thorough examination of the nose (possibly under anesthesia) will reveal the presence of a nasal foreign body. However, further tests, such as a nasal swab or flush and even X-ray or MRI of the nasal area, may be necessary.

Treatment Most dogs do well once the foreign body has been removed.

NASAL TUMORS

Nasal tumors, or polyps (benign masses), cause similar symptoms to nasal infections and foreign bodies.

?

What does it do
Respiratory system

The respiratory system consists of the nasal passages, larynx, trachea (windpipe), and lungs, as well as associated structures. It is involved in transporting air into and out of the body and enabling blood to carry oxygen to – and remove carbon dioxide from – the tissues.

THE RESPIRATORY SYSTEM

Air passes in through the nasal passages, then through the larynx, passing the vocal cords to travel down the trachea and into the lungs.

Air movement in and out of the lungs is controlled by movements of the chest wall and diaphragm, stimulated by nerve impulses from the brain.

The lungs lie on either side of the heart.

Trachea

The heart is positioned in the middle of the chest.

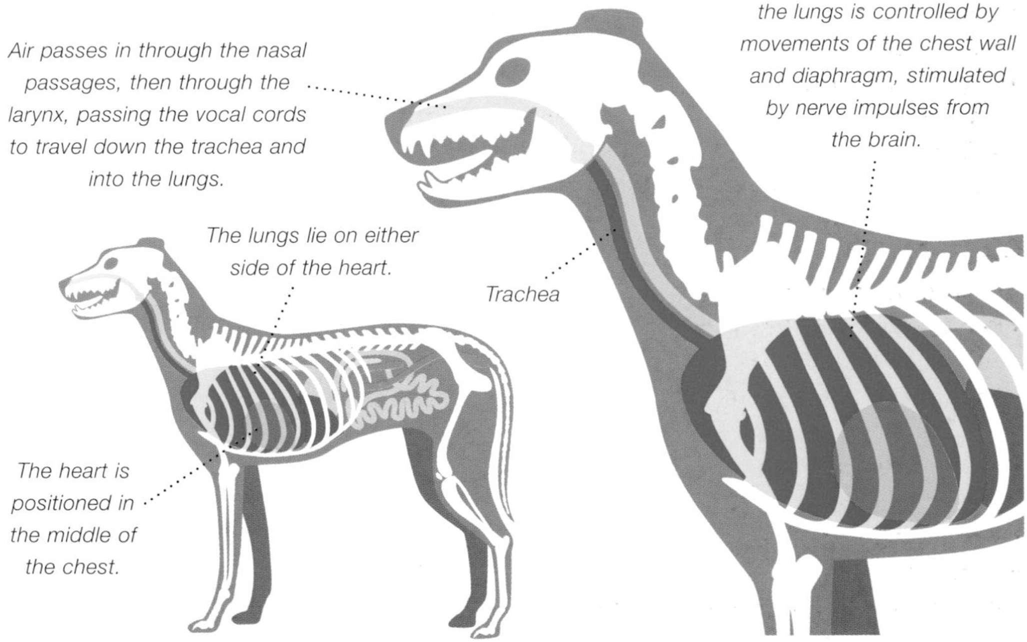

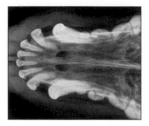

Left: Disease in the nasal passages may show up as loss of clarity on X-rays. This one shows no sign of health problems.

Symptoms

• Sneezing, nose bleeds, and episodes of nasal discharge may be evident.

Diagnosis X-rays, endoscopy, or even MRI may be needed to make a diagnosis. Examining a biopsy sample taken via an endoscope may aid identification of the exact type of tumor and thus the most appropriate treatment.

Treatment Outcomes vary depending on the type of tumor and whether or not it can be easily removed.

NASAL AND SINUS INFECTIONS

Symptoms

• Nasal discharge.

• Dogs may also feel unwell, have a high temperature, be unwilling to eat, and show signs of nasal pain.

• Bacterial, viral, and fungal infections may also be involved.

Diagnosis Laboratory examination of a nasal swab may allow a diagnosis to be made.

Treatment Viral infections may not require treatment, or the affected dog may only need supportive treatment, such as anti-inflammatory medication to help control fever and pain.

Antibiotics are used to treat bacterial infections. Fungal infections are harder to treat. Although oral antifungal medicines are effective in some cases, medication may need to be given directly into the affected sinuses via tubes while the dog is anesthetized.

LARYNGEAL PARALYSIS

If the larynx becomes partially or completely paralyzed, it no longer opens properly for each breath and instead blocks part of the affected dog's airway. Although this condition can occur in dogs of any age, it is seen most commonly in large breed older dogs with underlying diseases, such as **hypothyroidism** or **myasthenia gravis**.

Symptoms

• Affected dogs tend to tolerate exercise less.

• The tone of their bark may change and they often start to make a whistling noise as they breathe in.

Below: Older large breeds are susceptible to laryngeal paralysis. It can cause breathlessness, weakness after exercise, and coughing.

- Other symptoms include weakness after exercise, a bluish color of the mucous membranes (indicating insufficient oxygen in the system), coughing, and breathlessness.
- Dogs may also have trouble swallowing and eating and may choke or cough during and after eating.

Treatment Some dogs experience this condition mildly, with few symptoms, and need no treatment. In other cases, surgery (known as a tie-back) may be necessary to open up the larynx. In an emergency situation, affected dogs may need to be given extra oxygen and may also need a tracheostomy.

TRACHEAL COLLAPSE

The trachea, or windpipe, that carries air from the mouth and nose to the lungs is supported by a series of cartilage rings. In some dogs, particularly toy breeds, these cartilage rings are weak or malformed and the trachea can collapse inward. This prevents airflow, particularly when the dog takes large breaths, thus increasing the pressure within the trachea.

Symptoms

- Affected dogs may gasp, cough, and even collapse when excited or during exercise, especially if they wear a collar and pull on a leash.

Treatment Medication may reduce tracheal inflammation in affected dogs, and it is a good idea to use a harness rather than a collar. However, some affected dogs benefit from

What is
Tracheostomy

A tracheostomy is used for some forms of laryngeal disease, such as laryngeal paralysis and laryngeal cancer. An opening is made through the skin, directly into the windpipe so that affected dogs breathe through a hole in their neck rather than through the mouth/nose. Never let a dog with a tracheostomy swim – he will be unable to prevent water from flooding into the lungs and will drown.

surgery to strengthen the trachea and prevent it from collapsing.

KENNEL COUGH

Symptoms of acute tracheobronchitis, or kennel cough, include:

- Nasal discharge.
- A recurrent harsh cough.
- Tenderness and swelling of the lymph nodes in the neck.
- Sensitivity of the throat, so that it is painful when touched. Palpating the throat often induces coughing.
- Dogs may also have a high temperature and be unwilling to eat.

Diagnosis Kennel cough can be caused by several bacterial and viral infections, most notably *Bordetella* bacteria, **adenovirus** and parainfluenza virus (against which vaccines are available), and **herpes virus**. The infective agents present can be identified using nasal swabs and blood tests, although this is not always necessary.

Treatment Most dogs respond well to antibiotic treatment if there are signs of bacterial infection, and anti-inflammatory and antitussive medicines may also be used. It may take several weeks for dogs to recover completely, particularly from the viral elements of this condition.

Bronchial disease

A number of conditions can affect the bronchi (the airways within the lungs). Some old dogs develop chronic bronchitis, resulting from long-term inflammation of the bronchi, so that the bronchial walls become thickened and less elastic.

Symptoms
• A recurrent harsh cough that may be

? **What is**
Radiation therapy

Radiation therapy, or radiotherapy, is a form of treatment that involves passing a radioactive beam through abnormal tissues. This kills cells, particularly those growing and dividing fast, such as cancer cells.

accompanied by occasional retching of froth.
• Collapse may accompany severe coughing attacks.

Bronchiectasis, or swelling of the ends of the bronchi, may also develop as a consequence of many long-term respiratory diseases and can also result in a chronic cough.

Diagnosis In both cases, X-rays and possibly endoscopy of the bronchi may be required to make a diagnosis.

Treatment includes anti-inflammatory medication, bronchodilators, and antibiotics if bacterial infection is present.

ALLERGIC BRONCHITIS
Symptoms
• A chronic cough caused by inhaling allergens. Fungal and bacterial allergens may be involved, but inhaled pollens and dusts can also cause this kind of reaction.

Diagnosis may involve X-rays, endoscopy of the airways, and examining fluid sampled from the airways.

Treatment Affected dogs may benefit from anti-inflammatory medicines, antihistamines, and bronchodilators. Immunotherapy may also be helpful.

BRONCHIAL FOREIGN BODIES
Dogs sometimes inhale fragments of toys, grass, seed awns, and food fragments, all of which can pass down into the bronchi, where they cause inflammation and pain and can contribute to

Above: *Smelling flowers may not be a good thing: inhalation of allergens can cause allergic bronchitis in dogs, resulting in a chronic cough.*

difficulty in breathing. Secondary infection of damaged areas is also common.

Symptoms
- Affected dogs generally develop a sudden onset harsh cough.
- Signs of breathing difficulty and malaise (possibly).

Diagnosis X-rays may be diagnostic in some cases, but other investigations such as endoscopy may also be needed.

Treatment Removing the foreign body in question may be possible using the endoscope. Surgical removal from the lungs may be necessary, though very difficult.

Lungworm

Several types of lungworm can cause problems in dogs. *Dirofilaria* and *Angiostrongylus* both affect the lungs and the heart (see page 133), while *Crenosoma* (widespread in the U.S. and also present in Europe) and *Oslerus* specifically inhabit the lungs. *Oslerus* parasites develop within the bronchi and the tissues of the lungs; they are coughed up and then swallowed, migrating through the bowels and back to the lungs. *Crenosoma* has a similar life cycle, except that it involves a phase that takes place in slugs and snails that ingest larvae from dogs' feces. These develop and are passed back to dogs when they eat infected molluscs. The worms in the lungs cause inflamed nodules, thickened airways, inflammation, and sometimes a physical obstruction of the airway.

Symptoms
- A harsh cough.
- Breathing difficulties.
- Nasal discharge.

Diagnosis is possible following laboratory examination of the feces of affected dogs. Blood tests, X-rays, and endoscopy may also be helpful.

Treatment involves antiparasitic medicines, often for prolonged periods.

Pneumonia

Inflammation or infection of the lung tissue is referred to as pneumonia. If the bronchi are also involved, the disease is called bronchopneumonia. Pneumonia can result from infections, particularly in unwell or aged dogs and those that have trouble swallowing (or that have laryngeal paralysis), as they may inhale food that can set up infection. Dogs with heart conditions and excessive fluid in the lungs are also susceptible. Smoke inhalation may also predispose dogs to pneumonia.

Symptoms

- Affected dogs commonly cough and have difficulty breathing.
- Dogs may also be unwell, have a high temperature, and be unwilling to eat.

Diagnosis Auscultation (listening with a stethoscope) generally reveals crackly noises in the lungs. X-rays, together with laboratory examination of fluid from the lungs, can confirm the diagnosis.

Treatment In addition to antibiotics to fight bacterial infections (where present), anti-inflammatory medicines may be needed to help control the dog's temperature. Bronchodilators may assist its breathing.

PLEURAL FLUID/PYOTHORAX

Pleural fluid is fluid that builds up within the chest cavity in the space that surrounds the lungs. This fluid can prevent the lungs from inflating properly. Depending on the cause, different types of fluid may build up: blood may leak from damaged vessels after an injury (**chest trauma**) or pus may build up in the pleural space over a long period due to infection.

! Be aware

Paraquat

Paraquat, a herbicide, is palatable to dogs, and dogs may be poisoned after accidental ingestion, or over a long period of time following long-term exposure. It causes severe lung damage, as well as ulceration in the mouth and vomiting. Affected dogs rarely survive.

Symptoms

- Shallow, fast breathing.
- Breathlessness and coughing.

Diagnosis Examining chest X-rays may lead to a diagnosis, but blood tests and fluid analysis can also be helpful.

Treatment generally involves draining the offending fluid to allow the lungs to inflate properly and ease breathing, while the underlying problem is addressed.

Chest trauma

This commonly follows road traffic accidents and falls from a height.

Consequences

- Blood may leak into the pleural cavity.
- Lung injuries or punctures from fractured ribs can cause air to leak into the pleural space.
- Air may leak into the tissues under the skin, causing a crackly "bubblewrap"-type sensation to be felt when stroking an affected dog.

- Rupture of the diaphragm (the membrane that separates the chest and the abdomen), which contributes to a failure of the lungs to inflate normally.

Diagnosis X-rays, ultrasound scanning, and blood tests all aid diagnosis.

Treatment Collapsed lungs may need treatment to aid inflation, and dogs with rib injuries and chest pain may benefit from pain relief. Affected dogs may need oxygen therapy to help keep oxygen levels in the blood high enough in the immediate aftermath of an injury. Fluid or air may need draining from the chest to enable the lungs to inflate, and medicines may be prescribed to relieve pain, aid breathing, and treat or prevent the infection that commonly follows injuries that are contaminated and bruised. Injuries may require surgical repair once the dog's situation has been stabilized.

Lung tumors

A number of types of cancer have a tendency to spread via the blood (metastasize). Those that do so very often spread first to the lungs, so this is one of the first sites where metastatic tumors may be found. **Mammary tumors** in unneutered female dogs commonly spread by this route. In addition, some primary tumors may be located in the lungs.

Symptoms

- Coughing and breathlessness.
- It may be possible to detect quiet or dull areas in the chest when listening with a stethoscope.

Diagnosis X-rays are generally required. Endoscopy and ultrasound scanning may also be helpful.

Because the lungs are a predilection site for metastatic tumors, survey X-rays of the lungs are commonly taken when assessing cancer patients. These help establish the spread of the disease and determine whether or not the tumor has spread from its initial site.

Treatment Surgical removal of masses in the lungs is rarely an option, though radiation therapy and chemotherapy are sometimes used. In most cases, treating dogs with lung tumors is aimed at palliative care, rather than cure.

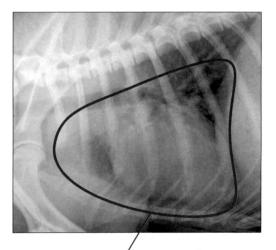

Patchy areas of consolidation on chest X-rays can indicate lung disease or tumors.

Eye problems

The eyes are particularly vulnerable to disease and injury, and eye problems are common. The function of the eyelids is to protect the eyes from injury, allowing them to remain healthy. Thus, eyelid disease or injury can cause secondary problems within the eyes and needs prompt veterinary attention.

The tear film plays an important role in keeping the eyes clean and well lubricated, and any disease in the tear system can also be problematic. Disease or damage of the conjunctiva (the membranes around the eyes) can obscure vision and this, too, can contribute to ocular pain and inflammation. Symptoms of eye disease are generally easy to detect.

Symptoms

- Swelling in or around the eye and discoloration of the eyes.
- Obvious wounds or injuries to the structures of the eye or the eyelids, as well as the development of a discharge from the eyes.
- Loss of transparency of the front part of the eyes; loss of the moistness and clarity of the eyes that can follow diminished tear production.
- Changes in the coloration of the surface of the eye, which can follow inflammation or damage.
- Inflammation may lead to pigmented deposits being laid down on the front surface of the

eye, resulting in a gritty, brownish appearance.
- Whitish or opaque scars can result from injury.
- Eye diseases can be very painful, and affected dogs often try to rub and scratch at their eyes, causing skin damage, hair loss, and inflammation of the facial skin in the eye area.

Diagnosis

Diagnosis requires a thorough examination.
- The eyelids and external ocular structures are assessed first and then the veterinarian uses an ophthalmoscope to examine the internal structures of the eye. In this way it is possible to assess the clarity of the front chamber and the lens and to check the back chamber of the eye and the retinal surface.

Above: *Damage to any of the parts of the eye leads to inflammation and changes in the blood circulation supplying those areas. This can cause a lack of transparency in the eye, which may be temporary or permanent and can affect vision.*

HOW THE EYE WORKS

Pupil

Light passes through the cornea and the front chamber, which is filled with clear fluid.

Lens

The clear cells of the cornea have no direct blood supply and receive nutrients from the fluid in the front chamber of the eye.

Iris (colored part of the eye)

Light focused by the lens passes through the back chamber of the eye to form an image on the retina.

Light-sensitive receptors in the retina generate nerve impulses that travel to the brain via the optic nerve.

- Schirmer tear test strips can measure tear production and check that dogs are producing sufficient quantities of tears. Fluorescein dye can then be instilled into the eyes. This is taken up by any damaged cells on the clear cornea, so that they appear bright green and can be assessed for size and depth of injury. Fluorescein also dissolves in the tear film, which should drain out of the eye into the nose without overflowing down the face. The veterinarian can then assess whether or not this system is working properly.
- Local anesthetic drops can be instilled into the eye, allowing for a more thorough examination of the eyes and ocular membranes. This can be particularly helpful if the veterinarian suspects that a foreign body, such as a grass seedhead, has become lodged behind the third eyelid or within a fold of conjunctival membrane.
- Finally, the pressure of fluid within the eye can be measured to identify glaucoma (increased ocular pressure) in affected animals. Ultrasound scanning and examination under general anesthesia can also be helpful.

Treatments

- Topical medicines (those applied directly to the area) may be used to treat infection, reduce pain and inflammation, and lubricate the eyes if they have inadequate tear production.
- Systemic (oral or injected) medicines may also be needed in some cases.
- Surgical treatment may be necessary to treat some injuries or to remove masses. Eyes are fragile organs that may be slow to heal. Prompt, effective treatment is particularly important when eye injuries are suspected. Be sure to seek veterinary advice.

Left untreated, eye conditions can become resistant to treatment, and the final course of action in a non-visual, painful, and untreatable eye may be to remove it surgically. Although the prospect of this is often very distressing for owners, dogs cope well with one eye or with a gradual loss of vision when this cannot be avoided.

Eyelid and eye surface problems

The eyelids should meet across the eye so that as the dog blinks, they clear the surface of the eye and spread the tear film across it to lubricate it. Eyelid abnormalities may prevent this from happening properly.

Above: A veterinarian uses an ophthalmoscope to carry out a thorough examination of the eyes and surrounding structures to check for problems.

CONFORMATIONAL ABNORMALITIES

Dogs with conformational abnormalities, common in certain breeds, may be unable to blink effectively or to lubricate their eyes sufficiently and they will be particularly prone to eye problems. Breeds with bulgy eyes, such as Pugs and Pekingese dogs, are particularly affected. Some breeds have lax (ectropion) or inturned (entropion) eyelids that cannot function effectively. Some Spaniels and Saint Bernards are affected with ectropion. Similarly, diamond eye (where the middle of the eyelid sags out and the corners turn in) may affect some dogs, such as Basset Hounds, while some Bulldogs and Shar Peis, among other breeds, experience entropion.

WARTS

With old age in any breed comes an increasing predisposition to warts.

Symptoms

- Warts sometimes develop on the eyelids, starting as a tiny mass on the edge of the eyelid. These can grow to the point where they start to rub and damage the eye surface.
- Secondary ocular swelling and discharge may be seen.

Treatment The wart may need removing by excising a wedge-shaped piece of eyelid.

EYELID INJURIES

Scratches and cuts may lead to eyelid swelling and loss of the smooth edge of the normal eyelid. If not treated appropriately, an irregular

- A mucus or pus-containing discharge.
- Corneal inflammation may follow, and the front surface of the eye may appear cloudy.

Treatment Bacterial or viral infection may be involved. Antibacterial eye drops may be needed.

OCULAR FOREIGN BODIES

Grass seed heads are a frequent problem in summer, as they can become lodged in the corner of the eye or under the third eyelid and may be difficult to see. Cat claws, thorns, and fragments of dirt or sticks can also cause problems.

Symptoms
- Swelling and pain.
- Ocular discharge.

Diagnosis Any dog with a swollen, painful eye should be thoroughly examined to ensure that no foreign body is present. This may be possible after applying anesthetic eye drops, but general anesthesia may be required for some dogs.

eyelid edge may result, predisposing the dog to future ocular disease.

Stings from bees and wasps commonly affect the facial area and may involve the eyelids, causing swelling. Other common causes of eyelid swelling include allergic disease, which can also cause conjunctivitis.

CONJUNCTIVITIS

Inflammation of the conjunctival membranes of the eye is known as conjunctivitis.

Symptoms
- Swelling and reddening of the membranes on the inside of the eyelids and surrounding the eyes.

Below: Dry eye, resulting from lack of tear production, causes inflammation of the eye surface, resulting in opacity across the cornea.

DRY EYE (KERATOCONJUNCTIVITIS SICCA)

Tear glands within the eyelids manufacture tears that constantly spread across the surface of the eyes, keeping them clean and lubricated. Loss of tear production due to disease of the tear gland results in a "dry eye."

Symptoms

- The eye loses its luster and becomes prone to inflammation and reddening.
- A sticky mucus discharge often develops.
- Over time, the front surface of the eye may become damaged and discolored, losing its transparency, which in turn leads to deterioration in vision.

Diagnosis Tear test strips can measure tear production over one minute, indicating whether or not a dog has "dry eye."

Treatment Affected dogs may benefit from ocular lubricants and anti-inflammatory or immune-modulating eye drops. Surgery to divert some flow of saliva to the eyes can be helpful in certain cases.

TEAR OVERFLOW

Certain breeds, particularly those with squashed faces such as Lhasa Apsos and Shih Tzus, may have narrowing or blockage of the nasolacrimal duct, which drains excess tears from the corner of the eye down to the nose. This condition can also result from facial injuries and from severe conjunctivitis.

Symptoms

- An overflow of tears onto the hair at the corner of the eyes, with consequent brown staining of the fur.

Diagnosis Fluorescein instilled into the eyes does not drain out at the nose as it should, confirming this condition.

Treatment Surgical treatment can improve matters; the opening of the nasolacrimal duct can be enlarged, or the duct can be flushed through until any blockages are clear.

EYE DAMAGE

Damage to the front surface of the eye can result from the presence of a foreign body, but it can also follow an injury such as a cat scratch.

Below: Tear overflow may cause brown staining of the fur below the inner corners of the eyes, here showing up clearly in this Lhasa Apso.

Above: Fluorescein dye shows the damaged area on the front of this dog's eye, not visible as an ulcer until the dye had been applied.

Symptoms

- A swollen, painful eye, which may be discolored or appear opaque.
- Injuries to the white of the eye (the sclera) may result in obvious reddening or bruising in this area.
- Injuries that affect the clear part of the front of the eye (the cornea) may be hard to see.

Diagnosis Fluorescent dye drops may outline damaged areas so that they can be assessed thoroughly.

Treatment In most cases, medication to lubricate the affected eye may be all that is needed to allow healing. However, some dogs develop infections that require treatment with antibiotic eye drops, while others benefit from surgery to encourage healing of the front surface of the eye. Clear contact lenses may also support and protect this area.

The front surface of the eye can be slow to heal because it contains no direct blood supply, relying instead on diffusion of nutrients from the fluid in the front chamber. For wounds or ulcers to heal, blood supply has to first grow across the front surface of the eye to the injury. Then, when the injury has healed, the blood vessels recede, leaving a transparent, or near-transparent cornea. Shallow injuries may heal completely within a matter of days, but deeper injuries can take longer, particularly if infection is involved. A slightly opaque scar can result, which may affect vision. Injuries that are slow to heal may benefit from surgical repair or surgical stimulation to inflame or damage the surrounding tissue, as this can stimulate healing. This may necessitate general anesthesia.

Above: Eye pain can cause blinking and aversion to bright light. Using an inappropriate shampoo on this Bichon Frise caused inflammation.

Disease within the eye

Injuries can cause bleeding into the globe of the eye.

Symptoms

- A reddened appearance of the inside of the eye that may obscure the ordinary appearance of the iris.
- Bleeding may also occur in the back part of the eye.
- Infection of the eye can lead to pus developing within the eye.
- Infection behind the eye can cause an abscess to develop that pushes the eye outward, so that it develops a more bulgy appearance.

Diagnosis Examination with an ophthalmoscope or more specialized equipment to measure the pressure in the eyes and to image structures in more detail. Ultrasound scanning allows the internal structures to be assessed thoroughly.

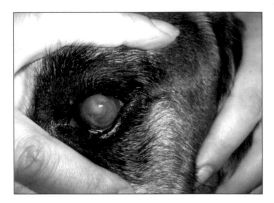

Above: Abnormal appearance of the eye consistent with a tumor. Seek prompt treatment.

Treatment Many eye diseases respond to topical drops, creams, or ointments. Others require systemic (via the body) treatment with antibiotics or anti-inflammatory medicines.

GLAUCOMA

Increased pressure within the eye is known as glaucoma. Swelling of the eye due to glaucoma or infection within the eye can be extremely painful.

Symptoms

- The eye swells, leading to a more bulgy appearance.
- Affected dogs often scratch at their eye or try to rub it on the ground.

TUMORS

Tumors within the eye can also cause changes in appearance and may lead to eye swelling.

> **!** Did you know
> ## Blindness
>
> *Dogs that lose vision generally cope well, even if they become profoundly blind. As long as they are taken on familiar walks and are kept on a leash near roads and other dangerous areas, they can continue to enjoy life. They can learn to play with audible toys and often run and play with a sighted companion.*

What is
Enucleation

Although appropriate medication and pain relief may assist the management of eye infection and injuries, some dogs with disease within the eye benefit from having the affected eye removed (enucleation). Although some owners worry about the aesthetics of such a procedure, dogs can cope well with a single eye.

Above: Enucleation (eye removal) is a salvage procedure. Having had one eye removed due to disease, this puppy is living a perfectly happy life.

CATARACTS

Cataracts sometimes occur in young dogs but are more common in older individuals.

Symptoms
- Opacity of the lens.
- Diminishing vision.

Treatment Hereditary cataracts in young dogs may be removed, leading to an improvement in vision. Most old-age cataracts, however, relate to aging within the eye that also affects other structures, so that there is rarely a benefit to removing "old-age" cataracts.

Crystalline "sugar" cataracts may also develop in dogs with **diabetes mellitus**, so any dogs that develop cataracts, drink excessively, and seem unwell should be checked out promptly.

Right: These telltale symptoms may indicate a tumor or abscess in the eye.

RETINAL DISEASE

This condition may occur as a hereditary problem in some dogs, leading to progressive loss of vision.

Diagnosis Genetic tests are available to check prospective parent dogs before breeding. Dogs from susceptible breeds should have their eyes inspected and certified before they are bred.

Neurological diseases

Neurological symptoms can result from disease in the brain, spinal cord, or peripheral nerves. Diseases elsewhere in the body can also cause neurological symptoms.

Hormonal conditions can cause neurological symptoms; **diabetes** is particularly commonly associated with neurological disease. Potentially, it can cause symptoms such as loss of consciousness, although it may also cause other signs, such as reduced nerve sensitivity.

Disorders of the **liver** and **kidney** can both cause toxin levels in the blood to rise, leading to neurological disease, such as weakness, wobbliness, and even seizures.

Symptoms

Neurological diseases can cause a range of symptoms including:

• Loss of vision, hearing, and appetite, collapse, limb weakness, lameness, wobbliness, pain, and loss of consciousness.

• Anxiety, aggression, and other changes in behavior.

• Some symptoms, such as mild or intermittent lameness, may be subtle and difficult to distinguish from other diseases or they may be overwhelming and obvious, such as seizures and loss of consciousness.

THE NERVOUS SYSTEM

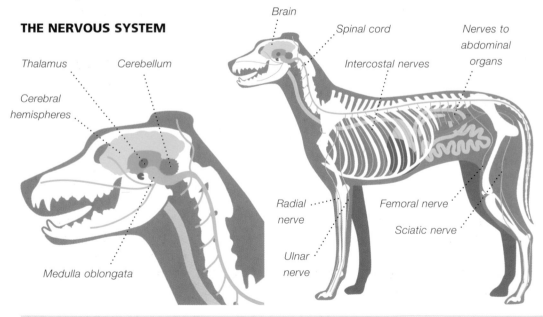

Brain

Spinal cord

Nerves to abdominal organs

Intercostal nerves

Thalamus

Cerebellum

Cerebral hemispheres

Radial nerve

Femoral nerve

Sciatic nerve

Ulnar nerve

Medulla oblongata

Diagnosis

Diagnosing neurological diseases generally necessitates a thorough neurological examination to check the following:

- Can the dog see and follow movement with his eyes? Can he smell and take, chew, and swallow food normally?
- Tests can also be done to check nerve function. Can the dog feel the skin on his face, trunk, and limbs? Can he can move his skin normally in response to a stimulus?
- Are the spine and limbs mobile? Is there pain? Reflexes indicate that the nervous system is working well.
- Internal organs need a normal nerve supply in order to function. Is the nerve supply to the bladder and bowel working properly? Otherwise, incontinence could result.

Treatments

Treatments vary depending on the cause of the problem.

- Antibiotics can treat infections.
- Both non-steroidal and steroid anti-inflammatory medicines can treat inflammatory disease.
- Neuroactive medicines can change or assist neurotransmission and enable nerves to function more normally.
- Supplementary antioxidants can remove toxins from the system, which may improve brain function.
- Surgical treatment is appropriate for some cases, but sadly, damaged or severed nerves

What does it do
The nervous system

The nervous system consists of the brain, spinal cord, and peripheral nerves. Together, they control thought, behavior, and both conscious and unconscious movement. Touch, taste, hearing, vision, smell, and pain are sensed by receptors in the skin and other tissues, which send messages to the brain and spinal cord.

Pain can result in a reflex unconscious movement (such as withdrawing from heat) due to connections made in the spinal cord that do not involve input from the brain or the transmission of information to the brain. However, most information is carried via the spinal cord to the brain, where it is processed. Then impulses travel back down the spinal cord to cause muscle contraction and conscious movement, such as choosing to lie down. The brain controls conscious movement in this way, but parts of it also control unconscious movements, such as breathing. Other pathways in the spinal cord carry information on coordination and balance.

cannot usually be repaired, although this is a current area of research and study.

Although some dogs recover from neurological disease, for many it may become chronic and cause an ongoing problem. Medication is aimed at keeping the brain and peripheral nervous system as healthy as possible, and minimizing symptoms for as long as possible.

Central nervous system (CNS) disorders

Diseases of the CNS may cause changes in behavior, plus loss of balance and coordination.

"STROKE" / CVA (CEREBRAL VASCULAR ACCIDENT)

Strokelike episodes can occur in dogs following a sudden lack of blood supply to a part of the brain (possibly due to blockage of a blood vessel by a fragment of fat, a tumor, a blood clot, or certain parasites). Alternatively, a blood vessel may burst or leak due to **circulatory disease, kidney disease**, or the growth of a tumor in

that area of the brain. Hypertension (high blood pressure) can cause similar problems.

Symptoms include:

- Sudden loss of balance and distress, sometimes combined with vomiting. A temporary loss of consciousness may also occur.
- Affected dogs often have nystagmus (their eyes flicker from side to side), show a head tilt to one side, and, if able to stand, may lean or circle to the same side.
- It may be hard for dogs to eat or drink, as their tongue and lip function may also be affected.

Diagnosis In many cases an accurate diagnosis is not made, but imaging techniques, such as MRI or CT scans, can reveal the lesion that caused the problem. The veterinarian can then identify the cause of the disease and treat it.

Treatment Although there is often little that can be done in terms of treatment, certain medicines and food additives (e.g., antioxidants) are sometimes used to try to limit damage to affected areas of the brain and to promote an improvement in brain function.

Left: Border Collies have a higher-than-average incidence of epilepsy.

? What is a
Seizure

- *Partial or complete loss of consciousness.*
- *Loss of ability to stand.*
- *Lying on side, thrashing with limbs.*
- *Salivating.*
- *Possibly uncontrolled relieving of the bowels.*

Mild seizures may be seen in conscious animals that can stand, evident as repetitive tics or muscle movements.

Other medicines may be used to try to keep the brain as healthy as possible.

Many dogs make a partial or full recovery over the days that follow, are able to get back on their feet, start to eat unaided, and enjoy life again. However, future strokelike episodes may follow and may be increasingly severe.

SEIZURES

These can occur in very sick dogs as a consequence of a number of diseases, but they also occur in otherwise healthy dogs for no apparent reason. The latter condition, known as idiopathic epilepsy, tends to occur in young adult dogs and is most common in certain breeds, such as Border Collies. Although some dogs have a single seizure and then never another, many

affected dogs go on to have regular seizures for the rest of their lives. These may gradually become more frequent and severe. Mild, brief seizures may not necessitate treatment (see page 186 for advice on how to deal with a seizure).

Symptoms of severe seizure include:

- Complete loss of consciousness and collapsing to the floor.
- Thrashing with the limbs.
- Salivating and often losing bowel and bladder control.

Treatment Medication reduces inappropriate electrical activity in the brain and thus decreases the chance of seizures occurring. Potential side effects can be seen as a result of anti-epileptic medication, and dogs vary enormously in terms of the dose of medication they need. Regular blood testing is normally carried out to monitor

Below: Head tilt and facial drooping indicate a lesion on one side of the brain, e.g., after a CVA.

the level of the medicine in the affected dog's blood and to ensure that it is in the right range.

Dogs that seizure due to underlying health problems may be suffering from **low or high blood sugar levels, liver disease, kidney disease**, or underlying brain disorders, such as inflammatory brain disease or a tumor involving the brain.

LOSS OF BALANCE AND COORDINATION

Stroketype symptoms may also follow **inner ear infections and disease**, vestibular disease, meningitis, and inflammatory brain disease. Brain tumors may also cause these symptoms.

Symptoms
- Losing balance.
- Suddenly developing a head tilt and a wobbly, lopsided gait.

Diagnosis of the exact cause of disease can be tricky unless MRI scanning is available.

Treatment with antibiotics and anti-inflammatory medicines can be used when appropriate; many dogs make a partial or even full recovery.

Loss of balance and coordination may also occur without a head tilt. In affected dogs it may correspond to disease in the back part of the brain or even in the spinal cord.

Symptoms
- Dogs may find it difficult to place their limbs correctly and may weave or stumble.

- Dogs may also sway and appear weak and wobbly.

Diagnosis MRI or other imaging techniques are needed for diagnosis.

Treatment Affected dogs may respond to anti-inflammatory medication or antibiotics, depending on the cause of disease.

SYRINGOMYELIA

This disease occurs due to a mismatch in size between the brain and the contours of the skull. This is seen in some brachycephalic (short- or broad-headed) and toy breeds of dog, most commonly in Cavalier King Charles Spaniels. The consequence of the condition is that the back part of the brain bulges and is subjected to increased pressure in the area where the top of the spine connects to the skull.

Below: A head tilt may indicate disease in the vestibular system, which links sensors in the inner ear to a balance control center in the brain.

Above: *Recumbent dogs need nursing care to keep them as comfortable as possible.*

Symptoms
- Neck pain and repetitive scratching at the neck or ears.
- Hind limb weakness and poor hind limb coordination.

Diagnosis can be difficult unless MRI scanning is available.

Treatment may not be effective.

HYDROCEPHALUS
This sometimes causes neurological disease in young brachycephalic breed puppies that suffer from an accumulation of fluid in the brain.

Symptoms
- Limb weakness.
- Blindness.
- Seizures.
- Characteristic domed skull that bulges up above the eyes. Symptoms may worsen as the affected puppy grows and as the fontanelle closes. (The fontanelle is the opening present in the skull at birth. It fuses as the puppy grows).

How to treat
Recumbent dogs

Recumbent dogs (those unable to rise) need to be propped up on the sternum in a soft comfy bed and moved from one side to the other every two to three hours if they are unable to maintain a sternal position. You may need to lift them outside for them to relieve themselves and clean them afterwards. They may need to be hand-fed with tasty morsels, or you may have to mash their food and feed them using a syringe. Canned fish and other foods with a strong smell help tempt dogs best, and heating food promotes odor and palatability. Severely affected dogs may need to be hospitalized, fed intravenously, and even catheterized to support them until their health improves.

Treatment Surgical treatment can be carried out to shunt fluid away from the brain, or medication may be used to reduce inflammation and to try to control seizures.

Spinal disorders
Spinal disorders can cause limb weakness, poor coordination, and pain in dogs that have normal brain function and behavior.

WOBBLER DISEASE

Cervical spondylopathy, also called wobbler disease, involves malformation of the vertebrae in the neck, resulting in compression of the spinal cord in this region. Dobermans, Dalmatians, and Bernese Mountain Dogs may have a genetic predisposition to this condition, which may occur most often in fast-growing individuals. It can also occur in toy breeds, such as Chihuahuas.

Symptoms include:

- Weak and wobbly hind legs and gait abnormalities of the front legs that may incorporate a high-stepping movement.
- Neck pain may also (rarely) be a feature and lifting the head can cause collapse, as it puts pressure on the affected area.

Diagnosis X-rays, myelograms (X-rays taken after a dye is injected into the spinal cord), and MRI scanning may be needed for an exact diagnosis.

Treatment may consist of anti-inflammatory pain-relieving medicines. Surgical stabilization of the affected area may also be helpful.

DISC DISEASE

Common in small dogs with long backs, such as Dachshunds, intervertebral disc disease occurs fairly frequently in older dogs. The condition involves part of the intervertebral disc moving and putting pressure on the spinal cord. This may occur due to a sudden injury or because of chronic disc disease that results in disc calcification. Minerals laid down within the disc make it less elastic.

Symptoms

- Back pain and stiffness.
- Dog may be unable to move well or jump.
- Prolapsed discs can also put pressure on emerging nerve roots as they leave the spinal cord, leading to loss of peripheral nerve function. This can cause nerve pain, as well as limb and back weakness and loss of reflexes in affected areas.

Be aware
Chocolate poisoning

Theobromine doses as low as 115 mg/kg of body weight have been reportedly fatal in dogs, although it usually takes at least twice this amount. Since dark chocolate contains around 15 mg/gm of theobromine, as little as 8 gm of dark chocolate per kg body weight could be fatal. Keep chocolate away from dogs. Symptoms of chocolate poisoning include seizures and increased heart and breathing rates. Affected dogs benefit from supportive treatment and medication to reduce further absorption of the toxin if they have been recently exposed. Some dogs make a full recovery, but those that eat a large amount may suffer cardiovascular collapse and die.

An X-ray of the spine allows the veterinarian to assess disc spaces.

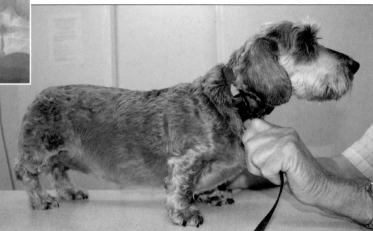

Right: Old Dachshunds are particularly prone to disc disease.

- In the most severe cases, affected dogs lose mobility in some or all of their limbs and may also lose sensation. In addition, they may lose the ability to pass urine and feces normally, and permanent nerve damage can result. Discospondylitis may also occur. This involves infection of the disc material and can cause similar symptoms.

Diagnosis generally requires X-rays and, in some cases, MRI. This allows imaging of the affected disc and enables the veterinarian to exclude other diseases that cause similar symptoms, such as spinal tumors and **FCE** (fibrocartilagenous embolism). MRI scanning also allows assessment of the spinal cord.

Treatment with anti-inflammatory medicines, combined with strict rest, may enable affected discs to settle down and become less painful and swollen. This can result in a decrease in the pressure being put on the spinal cord and an improvement in limb function. However, in some cases, surgical intervention to remove prolapsed disc material may also be necessary.

Many affected dogs do well, although they may need special care to help avoid future symptoms of disc disease. They should avoid steps and jumps and should initially have fairly restricted exercise levels, although these may be built up gradually.

FCE (FIBROCARTILAGENOUS EMBOLISM)

FCE, also known as ischemic myelopathy, results when a fragment of intervertebral disc breaks away from a damaged disc and blocks the blood flow to a section of spinal cord. Fragments of fat or even tumor can block spinal arteries with similar effects. Lack of blood supply to the spine causes damage to that part of the spinal cord, with resultant loss of nerve supply from more distal areas (areas further from the brain).

Be aware
Strychnine poisoning

Some rodenticides contain the neurotoxin strychnine (others contain anticoagulants). Affected dogs may develop symptoms within minutes to hours of exposure (by eating rat poison). Symptoms include anxiety, nervousness, drooling, and muscle spasm, which develops into seizures. Analysis of vomit or a history of access to poison can confirm the disease, but emergency treatment is generally started as symptoms develop. Medication is given to reduce further absorption of the toxin and to try to control seizures. Intravenous fluids are beneficial. Dogs are kept in a quiet, darkened room to reduce stimulation and breathing, and the heart is monitored in case further treatment is necessary. The poison runs its course in twenty-four to forty-eight hours; dogs that survive this period generally recover well.

Symptoms

- Depending on the part of the spinal cord that is affected, dogs may suddenly become paralyzed in one, two, or four limbs to varying degrees. Typically, the condition is not painful.

Diagnosis can be tricky, as even with specialized imaging techniques such as MRI, it can be impossible to detect the cause of disease. However, X-rays and MRI can allow other causes of similar disease to be excluded, such as disc disease and spinal tumors and **fractures** (although the latter are extremely painful, unlike FCE). Diagnosing FCE may be possible only when a section of spine is examined microscopically at post-mortem examination.

Treatment No specific treatment exists to aid healing in this condition. Supportive care and physiotherapy can help affected dogs to be comfortable and maintain strength in paralyzed limbs. Over time, a proportion of dogs (especially those that retained paw sensation in affected limbs) will regain some or all of their strength, but sadly some dogs never recover.

DM (DEGENERATIVE MYELOPATHY)

DM, also known as CDRM (chronic degenerative radiculo myelopathy), involves progressive damage affecting the nerves that supply the hind limbs in affected dogs. A hereditary predisposition is present in some German Shepherd Dogs (and a DNA test for this now exists), but other large and giant breeds may also be affected.

Symptoms

- Dogs gradually lose hind limb function but suffer no pain.
- Often, they progress from lifting their feet up less well to brushing or dragging the hind feet (wearing down the claws as a consequence). Loss of hind limb function, collapse, and inability to rise follow.

Diagnosis is tricky because, as with ischemic myelopathy, there are no structural changes that can be imaged. Instead, nerve damage takes place at a cellular level and may not be picked up until post-mortem examination. However, X-rays and MRI scanning may be needed to exclude other similar conditions and allow this one to be diagnosed.

Treatment is not curative – the disease is inevitably progressive. However, there are some suggestions that Vitamin E supplementation may be helpful. Hydrotherapy and physiotherapy are advisable, as they allow dogs to maintain muscle and strength in their hind limbs for as long as possible, which helps them retain mobility. Some owners use mobility carts for affected dogs; the appropriateness of these depends on how individual dogs cope with them.

CAUDA EQUINA NEURITIS

This is an inflammatory disease of the nerves in the lower portion of the spine in the pelvis and tail area.

Symptoms

- Compression of the nerves in this region due to disc problems, spinal tumors, nerve inflammation, or infection causes pain and weakness in the pelvis, tail, and hind limb area.

Diagnosis Attempting to diagnose this condition is frustrating, as cases show inconsistent signs. However, imaging the affected area can help exclude other conditions, and blood tests can be done to check out some infectious causes of disease.

Treatment is generally ineffective, but hydrotherapy and physiotherapy help dogs to maintain strength and mobility for as long as possible.

Above: *German Shepherd Dogs and other large-breed dogs may develop degenerative myelopathy, causing progressive loss of hind limb function.*

Infectious neurological disease

A number of infections exist that can occasionally cause neurological disease.

TETANUS

Although rare in dogs, tetanus is an occasional cause of disease when *Clostridium tetani* bacteria from the soil enter the body in a deep, dirty wound. Although dogs are relatively resistant to this disease, the toxins produced can spread through the body, causing muscle spasm and paralysis. Initially, the symptoms are most obvious in the smallest muscles in the body.

Symptoms

• The face can become paralyzed, with the ears erect, the mouth curled into a "grin," and the third eyelid prolapsed so that it can be seen in the corner of the eye.
• Paralysis of respiratory muscles can follow, causing death.

Diagnosis can be difficult, but the signs of this condition are fairly definitive.

Treatment is not always successful, but affected dogs generally need supportive care in a quiet, darkened room to reduce muscle stimulation. They may need intravenous fluids and food delivered straight into the stomach by a gastrostomy tube. Antibiotics and tetanus antitoxins can be given. In some cases, the dog's breathing may also need supporting with a ventilator.

RABIES

Rabies is common in the wild animal population in many countries, but not present in the U.K., some other European countries, Japan, and Australasia. It results from a viral infection that is transmitted in the saliva of a bite from an infected animal. The disease is zoonotic (transmissible to humans), so if an infected animal bites a human that person can also catch it. Affected dogs may incubate the virus for months before symptoms are seen. Quarantine and the Pet Travel Scheme are in place in some countries to prevent affected animals from being imported.

Symptoms

• Fever.
• Pupillary dilation so that the eyes widen.
• Reddening of the eyes.

Below: Drooping of the eyelids and prominence of the third eyelid can indicate a focal neurological problem involving the facial nerves.

Above: *Contraction of facial muscles resulting in a worried expression may be a first sign of tetanus.*

- Changes in behavior.
- Dogs may become somnolent, weak, and paralyzed, or very aggressive.
- Excessive drooling.

Affected dogs should not be approached. Euthanasia is generally necessary, and tests are then carried out to confirm the disease. Vaccination against rabies may prevent this disease, but even vaccinated dogs can sometimes be affected.

DISTEMPER

Although common at one time, distemper is relatively rare now that many dogs are vaccinated against it.

Symptoms

- Unvaccinated dogs tend to develop a high temperature and non-specific signs of ill health, followed by respiratory disease, such as coughing and nasal discharge.
- Digestive disease – diarrhea and vomiting.
- Neurological signs, such as seizures. Incoordination, blindness, and tremors may develop.
- The pads of the feet may thicken, and affected pregnant females tend to lose their pregnancy.

Diagnosis is possible when blood samples are examined at the laboratory.

Treatment Little exists other than supportive care. A proportion of dogs may survive infection but many die, and a number of those that do survive have ongoing neurological signs.

TOXOPLASMOSIS AND NEOSPORA

Both these protozoal parasites can cause disease in many parts of the body, including the brain and spinal cord. Toxoplasmosis is also transmissible to humans.

Symptoms

- Weakness and paralysis.
- Dogs may develop skin rashes, muscle pain, heart disease, liver disorders, and general ill health.

Diagnosis Blood tests and samples of fluid from affected areas can be diagnostic.

Treatment Both diseases can be treatable in some cases if affected dogs are given long courses of appropriate medicines.

Bone, joint, and muscle problems

The symptoms of musculoskeletal disease are wide ranging. Lameness may vary from acute (sudden) onset non-weight-bearing lameness, generally relating to broken limbs or ruptured ligaments that result in joint disruption, to insidious onset (chronic) low-grade stiffness and reduced mobility that can result from osteoarthritis and degenerative joint disease.

Symptoms

- From lameness and pain to loss of the normal architecture of the body, resulting in the inability to rise or bear weight.
- Muscle wastage and weakness can also result.
- Affected areas may develop an abnormal contour due to swellings or to lack of congruency of bones within joints.
- Abnormal movement may lead to the development of skin disease or wounds in affected areas.

Diagnosis

First, the veterinarian must thoroughly examine the affected animal.

- Observing the dog while he is moving at a walk and trot helps the veterinarian determine the degree of lameness present and which leg – or legs – it is affecting. Subtle changes in the way the limb is used may indicate whether any stiffness is coming from the upper or lower limb, and whether or not any neurological problems, such as difficulty placing the limb correctly, or toe scuffing, are present.
- The next stage involves feeling (palpating) and manipulating affected areas to identify swollen, stiff, or painful joints and to locate the source of the pain causing lameness.

?

What does it do
Musculoskeletal system

The musculoskeletal system consists of the bones of the limbs, spine, ribs, and head, as well as the joints, ligaments, tendons, and muscles. Its most obvious function is to enable movement. However, it also provides the framework within which the organs and tissues function, while the rib cage protects the vital structures in the chest. So, while disease in the musculoskeletal system most commonly affects movement and causes symptoms such as lameness, weakness, and inability to bear weight on one or more limb(s), it can also have profound effects on other organ systems within the body.

THE MUSCULOSKELETAL SYSTEM

The bones provide the framework of the body, giving it strength and solidity.

Muscles are attached to bones by tendons. Contraction in different muscles pulls bones into various positions, enabling the limbs to move. Muscle contraction is initiated by nerve stimulation via the brain and spinal cord, therefore neurological diseases can mimic musculoskeletal problems.

Muscle contraction allows one bone to move relative to another, resulting in limb or spine movement.

The bones are joined together by ligaments that run from one bone to the next, holding them close together so that movement within a normal range can occur, and movement outside a normal, comfortable range is prevented.

Synovial membranes encapsulate joints and manufacture joint fluid, which acts as a lubricant and shock absorber within the joints.

Cartilage forms a smooth surface over bone ends within the joints, allowing the bone ends to glide smoothly across each other with minimal friction.

- X-rays are often helpful, as assessing the radio-density of the bones and associated structures can allow diagnosis of many types of musculoskeletal disease. Fractures can show up on X-rays as lines across bones or fragmentation of the outline of bones. Arthritic change can show up as irregularity of the contour of bones at the joints. Mineralized fragments can sometimes be seen in diseased soft tissues adjacent to joints and bones.
- Other types of imaging are needed to investigate diseases of the musculoskeletal

system that predominantly affect the soft tissues, such as muscles, tendons, ligaments, and the synovial membranes. Ultrasound scanning can be helpful, as can MRI, which shows both soft tissue and bone surfaces well. Nuclear scintigraphy may also be helpful. This involves injecting a non-toxic radioactive dye and using a special camera to detect the areas where the dye is concentrating because there are high levels of actively dividing cells. It can be useful for identifying diseased tissues.

Treatment

A number of types of treatment can be appropriate for dogs with musculoskeletal disease.

- Most commonly, non-steroidal anti-inflammatory medicines help reduce pain and inflammation associated with limb or back injuries or disease. Other classes of pain medicines, such as opiates (morphine-type) and local anesthetics, can also be used.
- Acupuncture can provide a potent source of pain relief in some animals.
- Other treatments include antibiotics to treat infection; steroids and other immune-modulating medicines to treat autoimmune disorders; and medicines that affect nerve transmission can be used to treat neurological conditions.
- Surgery can repair broken bones; replace or repair damaged ligaments and muscles; stabilize weakened or diseased structures; and remove damaged tissues.

> **!** Be aware
> ## Sudden fractures
>
> *Fractures sometimes occur unexpectedly in bones that are already weakened by a bone tumor. X-rays reveal the presence of a tumor as well as a fracture. Repair may not be possible; instead, treatment may incorporate limb amputation. This can allow dogs to return to a happy life, as long as tumors present have not already spread elsewhere in the body (metastasized).*

- Rest, controlled levels of gradually increasing convalescent exercise, and hydrotherapy can all enable damaged structures to heal and regain strength. Physiotherapy can also be useful. This involves massage and mobilization techniques, as well as exercises to assist dogs with impaired limbs and joints to maintain their mobility and reduce pain levels.

Acute injuries

Acute problems include those that occur as a consequence of accidents and injuries, such as broken bones; dislocated joints; and tendon, muscle, and ligament damage.

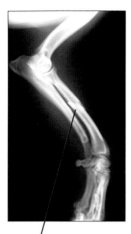

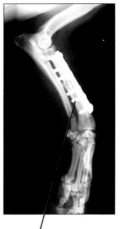

This dog has fractured its radius and ulna (in the forearm) while running after a ball.

Surgical repair with a metal plate stabilizes the fracture and allows it to heal.

FRACTURED OR BROKEN BONES

These generally occur as a sudden onset injury following an accident of some kind.

Symptoms

- Some fractures may remain non-displaced (i.e., the bone ends are still aligned) and may simply cause some pain and lameness.
- Others involve obvious disruption in the architecture of the affected area and can result in severe and non-weight-bearing lameness in misshapen, weak, and collapsing limbs.
- In the worst case, fractures may be associated with skin wounds and may, in such cases, be associated with contamination or infection of affected areas.

LIMB FRACTURES

These often result from road traffic accidents.

Symptoms

- Generally, the dog is suddenly unable to bear weight on a limb, usually after a known injury.
- The affected limb may be held up tight to the body or may appear to swing loosely.
- Fragments of bone may even penetrate the skin if wounds are present, so that the fragments are visible within the wound.
- If severe damage to blood vessels is present in the affected area, hemorrhage may also be a problem. In such cases it may be necessary to apply a pressure bandage (see page 191) to prevent or reduce blood loss.

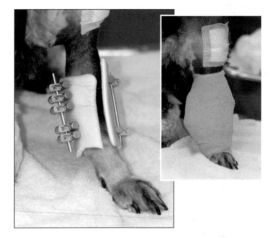

Above: *In some cases, where plating is not feasible, an external fixator is used to stabilize a fracture. Bandaging around the site ensures that the area is kept clean to prevent infection.*

Treatment It is usually best to seek urgent veterinary attention without attempting to bandage or splint the limb, as doing so can often cause unnecessary pain and distress and may be dangerous if dogs are in severe pain, as they may behave aggressively.

At the veterinary practice, the first step is to staunch any blood loss and then to assess the type and degree of injury. A thick supportive bandage may be applied to stabilize the fracture and prevent further injury to soft tissues in the area. Treatment is generally carried out under general anesthesia. Some fractures are best cast or splinted, while others require internal fixation/repair with screws and plates. Some fractures are so severe that they are irreparable, and limb amputation may need to be considered in some cases.

? What happens after **Amputation**

Amputation – the surgical removal of a limb – is sometimes carried out when severe fractures and limb injuries occur, or to treat certain types of cancer. Many dogs live happy and mobile lives on three legs, with surprisingly few problems. However, their remaining limbs are subjected to increased stresses and increased chance of injury.

RIB FRACTURES

Rib fractures can also follow accidents or injury.

Symptoms

- Forelimb lameness due to pain in the chest muscles adjacent to the forelimbs.
- Coughing, panting, and difficulty breathing.
- Signs of pain when breathing. Should a bone fragment penetrate deeper structures, such as the lungs, severe dyspnoea (breathing difficulty) may result, and air leakage from the lungs may also occur. If air comes to lie under the skin, it can result in a crackly "bubble wrap" texture in the skin.

Treatment Rib fractures rarely need to be repaired surgically. Most stabilize with time and need little treatment. However, fragments of bone may need to be removed, and leaked air may have to be drained, otherwise the lungs may be unable to inflate.

SPINAL FRACTURES

Road traffic accidents, falls from up high, and impact injuries that cause trauma can result in spinal fractures.

Symptoms

- Acute paraplegia (paralysis of the limbs) that may affect either just the hind limbs or all four limbs, depending on the location of the injury.

Treatment Surgical treatment to stabilize such fractures may be appropriate, but in most cases, spinal fractures occur concurrently with severe damage to the spinal cord. Many victims will not recover, so euthanasia may be recommended.

DISLOCATIONS

Dislocation of the hips is another relatively common acute onset injury that may follow a bump from a car affecting the hip area.

Symptoms

- Dogs are generally in significant pain and unable to bear weight on the affected limb.

Diagnosis Examination may reveal an asymmetric pelvis, and the head of the femur (the thigh bone) may be located in an abnormal position.

Treatment Under anesthesia it may be possible to relocate the limb, and X-rays should be taken to

Left: Despite having had a limb amputation, many dogs, such as this Lhasa Apso, can lead an active and happy life.

check that no other major injuries are present. As long as the joint capsule of the hip remains reasonably strong, the replaced hip may stay located in the acetabulum (socket) in the pelvis. However, severe damage to the surrounding structures may prevent the hip from staying located and may result in the dislocation recurring. Using a specialized bandage to support the joint may help the hip stay located, but surgery is often needed to repair the dislocation.

CRUCIATE LIGAMENT RUPTURE

The cruciate ligaments are located within the stifle (knee) joints, where they hold the femur and tibia in alignment, allowing the stifle joint to act like a hinge. Rupture of these ligaments contributes to joint laxity and allows the femur and tibia to move relative to one another in a way that contributes to pain and joint damage. Degenerative joint disease can result, manifested as **osteoarthritis**. **Arthritis** also contributes to weakening of the cruciate ligaments, which causes further damage. Affected dogs are generally overweight, large, and giant breed dogs in the later stages of their life. Low-grade cruciate ligament disease may cause few obvious symptoms, but once the ligaments are weakened they are easily damaged further.

Symptoms

• Often, the first sign of a problem is that an older dog suddenly cries out and becomes severely lame on a hind limb, often after a sudden jump or twisting movement.

Diagnosis may be possible during a basic clinical examination. Affected dogs have a swollen, painful stifle that may be sufficiently lax so that "drawer" (front-to-back movement of the tibia relative to the femur) is present. X-rays may show bone damage in the areas where the ligaments attach and may also reveal joint swelling. More specialized imaging techniques may also be necessary, but in most cases diagnosis is fairly straightforward.

Treatment Most dogs do best with surgical treatment to graft in a replacement ligament and/or to improve the alignment of bones within the joint and tighten up the joint to reduce laxity. Some smaller dogs will recover a proportion of their mobility without surgery, given a sufficient period of rest and medication to relieve inflammation and pain. Some dogs that have suffered a cruciate ligament injury on one hind limb will go on to injure the other in future.

? What are Nutraceuticals

Nutraceuticals are food supplements that have an effect on health. A number are gaining recognition as adjuncts in the treatment of a range of diseases. Examples include glucosamine (in joint disease) and sAME (in liver disease).

Above: *Older, overweight, large-breed dogs are particularly at risk for cruciate ligament disease.*

JOINT STRAIN

Overstretch injuries that affect joints can cause joint swelling and pain. This generally resolves with rest and anti-inflammatory medication.

Chronic and degenerative diseases

Chronic or degenerative bone and joint diseases can result from abnormal development of these structures, combined with low-grade damage over a long period of time. Resultant changes in mobility can be associated with chronic pain.

HIP DYSPLASIA

In this condition, the hip joint is abnormally shallow and lax, so that it does not fit together tightly. There is an inherited tendency to develop this condition, and dogs from affected breeds should be X-rayed and their hips assessed before breeding. Hip dysplasia-prone breeds include German Shepherd Dogs, Labrador and Golden Retrievers, Rottweilers, and giant breeds.

Being overweight, growing too fast, and over-exercise on immature joints can also predispose dogs to developing this condition. Hip dysplasia also predisposes to osteoarthritis, leading to hip stiffness and pain in older dogs. On examination, affected dogs generally have a reduced range of movement in their hips and may experience pain when their hips are manipulated.

Symptoms

- Hind limb weakness and lameness may be evident in young dogs.
- Affected dogs may simply exhibit a swinging gait, where their hindquarters sashay from side to side as they walk. A low, crouching hind limb gait may also be seen.

Diagnosis involves taking X-rays of the hips and assessing the laxity of the joints. Taking these factors into account, together with the severity of the dog's symptoms, the veterinarian can then assess the degree of the problem and the best course of treatment.

Treatment Dogs with severe hip dysplasia may

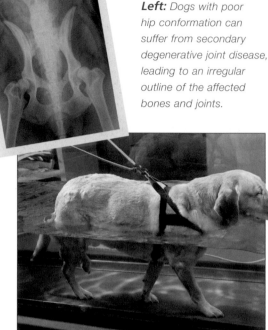

Left: Dogs with poor hip conformation can suffer from secondary degenerative joint disease, leading to an irregular outline of the affected bones and joints.

Above: Dogs with degenerative joint disease can benefit from hydrotherapy. Here, a Labrador with hip problems undergoes a session of hydrotherapy in a treadmill tank.

benefit from surgery to bring the hip joints into better alignment or even hip replacement surgery. In the long term, they – and dogs with milder disease – will benefit from controlled levels of regular exercise and judicious use of medication to relieve inflammation and pain. Physiotherapy and hydrotherapy to build up the supporting musculature may also be of value.

ELBOW DYSPLASIA

Malformation or abnormal development of the elbow joint, known as elbow dysplasia, also has a hereditary basis. X-rays of dogs can be taken to assess their elbows before they are used for breeding, and appropriate diet and exercise in young puppies may reduce the chance of problems occurring.

Symptoms

- As young, growing puppies, affected dogs may develop forelimb lameness and elbow swelling, or they may develop problems with secondary osteoarthritis in older age.
- Examination of affected dogs reveals stiff, painful, swollen elbows.

Diagnosis X-rays can allow bone fragments within the elbow joint to be identified.

Treatment Surgical treatment to remove bone fragments and help stabilize affected joints may be helpful in some dogs. In severe cases, elbow replacement surgery may even be an option. Affected dogs also benefit from suitable levels of exercise. Pain-relieving medication may be helpful, and hydrotherapy may aid mobility.

OSTEOCHONDROSIS

This refers to abnormal cartilage development, which can occur in large-breed dogs during growth. It is normally identified in young dogs. Osteochondrosis can affect the shoulders, elbows, and carpi (wrists) in the forelimbs, and the hocks and stifles (knees) in the hind limbs.

? *What is*
Hydrotherapy

During hydrotherapy, or water therapy, dogs are able to swim or walk or run on an underwater treadmill to encourage mobilization. It allows dogs with restricted mobility due to joint, limb, or back problems to exercise. Encouraging exercise while in a buoyant state helps maintain limb strength and mobility in dogs with orthopedic problems.

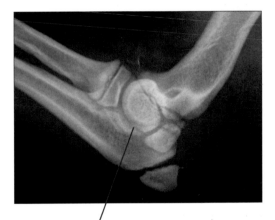

Abnormal elbow development can predispose to degenerative joint disease.

Symptoms

- Affected dogs generally have one or more swollen, painful joints and lameness, resulting from inflammation due to damaged cartilage.

Diagnosis X-rays may reveal affected areas of bone or cartilage damage, but more specialized imaging techniques, including ultrasound scanning and MRI, may be needed in some cases. Arthroscopy (scoping the joint with a tiny camera through a minute incision under general anesthesia) can allow more accurate identification of the exact structures involved.

Treatment such as removing damaged tissue can also be carried out during arthroscopy. Affected joints are predisposed to developing osteoarthritis in older age, and the disease

Above: *Small terrier breeds are predisposed to the development of Legg Perthes disease.*

What is...
Arthroscopy

Arthroscopy uses fiber optics to pass a tiny camera into a diseased joint through a minute incision. It is then possible to carry out microsurgery without opening up the whole joint. It can be used to treat damaged ligaments and cartilage and arthritic change.

may also show up in older animals due to joint pain and stiffness of this nature. In addition to arthroscopic treatment in some cases, rest and anti-inflammatory pain-relieving medication may be helpful.

Legg Perthes disease

This hereditary, degenerative condition of the hips is generally seen in miniature and toy breed dogs. It results in loss of blood supply to the top part of the femur, so that it crumbles away.

Symptoms

- Affected dogs of any age generally show signs of progressive hind limb lameness and stiffness, which is easily confused with arthritic change.
- Manipulating affected hips is painful.
- Crepitus (a feeling of roughness) is often present.

Diagnosis X-rays taken of the hips can confirm the presence of Legg Perthes disease.

Treatment Although gentle exercise and pain-relieving medicines can help affected dogs maintain their mobility, most do best with surgical removal of damaged tissue (excision arthroplasty), so that the shaft of the femur forms a false joint with the pelvis. Mobility after this operation can be aided by judicious use of pain-relieving medicines, together with physiotherapy and hydrotherapy.

PATELLAR LUXATION

Some small and toy breeds of dog are prone to patellar luxation. Typically associated with a "knee out" conformation that creates asymmetric stresses through the joint, this condition involves the patella, or knee cap, not fitting properly into the patellar groove on the base of the femur.

Symptoms

• As the stifle flexes or bends, the patella may leave its groove and lie medial to it (on the inside surface of the joint). This may happen at every stride or may be intermittent, depending on the severity of the problem. When it does occur intermittently, affected dogs often carry a hind limb for a couple of strides before bearing weight again.

Diagnosis may be possible following a thorough examination, as the patella may be felt slipping in and out of joint as the affected limb is manipulated. X-rays allow further assessment of the structure of the joint and the degree of associated arthritic change.

Treatment Depending on the diagnosis, either carefully controlled exercise levels and medication or surgery to realign the joint and set the patella more firmly into a deeper groove.

OSTEOARTHRITIS

Degenerative joint disease, or osteoarthritis, refers to the changes that can occur in normal joints with age, due to wear and tear. These changes are amplified in joints that have been injured or damaged, or that are poorly aligned, leading to an increase in stress applied to the structures of the affected joint.

Damage to the articular cartilage surfaces within the joints (the bits of bone that interact with each other) leads to an increase in inflammation within the joint. This in turn can lead to deposition of tiny bone fragments at the margins of the joint, as well as joint swelling and weakening of the supportive structures around

? What is...
Arthrodesis

Arthrodesis, or surgical fusion of joints, is another possible salvage procedure. It can reduce the pain associated with severe joint disease by stabilizing the affected joint and fusing it. Mobility is affected as the joint is fixed, but this procedure can aid pain management in some dogs.

the joint. The new bone fragments contribute to joint stiffness and inflammation. Over time, the range of motion of an affected joint becomes increasingly restricted. The dog experiences more pain and becomes more lame.

Symptoms
• Lameness and pain.
• Joint swelling and joint stiffness.

Diagnosis is possible following X-rays, which show the characteristic changes in bone density and new bone formation in and around the affected joint.

SPONDYLOSIS

Arthritic changes between the vertebrae of the spine, known as spondylosis, can also cause back pain and stiffness, as well as reduced peripheral nerve function.

Symptoms
• Affected dogs often develop a stiff immobile spine and may start to exhibit an arched and tense back.
• The dog may also find it hard to bend as it moves and may change gait as a consequence.
• Some dogs find pacing (where both legs on the same side move together) more comfortable than normal trotting.

Diagnosis generally necessitates X-rays. MRI and other imaging techniques may also be helpful.

Treatment Affected dogs generally benefit from anti-inflammatory pain-relieving medicines. Acupuncture and physiotherapy may also help.

OSTEOARTHRITIS

Fluid in the joints acts as a shock absorber. Arthritis reduces the viscosity of this fluid.

Cartilage damage and the deposition of mineral fragments within the joint cause progressive joint stiffness and pain.

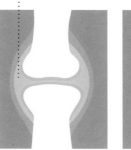
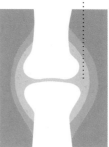

Below: *Acupuncture involves the use of fine sterile needles placed through the skin at particular points in the body where they can have an effect on the nervous system. It can be used to treat pain and muscle spasm.*

Rheumatoid and other forms of arthritis

Other forms of arthritis, or joint inflammation, include rheumatoid arthritis and immune-mediated arthritis, both of which can cause joint swelling, stiffness, and pain. However, these conditions do not relate to joint inflammation and new bone formation, but to the body making antibodies and immune chemicals that damage its own joint tissues.

Diagnosis may necessitate X-rays, but blood tests and tests on joint fluid from affected joints can also be helpful.

INFECTIOUS ARTHRITIS

Swollen, painful, inflamed joints can also result from infection. Bacterial infection can follow contamination of a wound in the region of a joint, and other infections in the body may settle out in damaged joints.

Symptoms
• A swollen, painful joint (as above), but affected dogs also often have a high temperature.

Diagnosis Blood tests and joint fluid tests can be helpful.

Treatment involves antibacterials or medicines that combat other types of infection.

LYME DISEASE

This is particularly common in parts of the world where the sheep and deer ticks that carry it are endemic. If an infected tick bites a dog it can transmit *Borrelia* (the pathogen that causes

> ### The use of
> # *Joint replacements*
>
> *Severely abnormal or arthritic joints may be replaced with a prosthetic joint as a salvage procedure to reduce pain. Hip replacements have been available for some time and provide a valuable option in the treatment of hip dysplasia and resultant degenerative joint disease. Newer procedures include elbow and stifle (knee) replacements.*

X-rays of the spine in the region of the chest reveal signs of spondylosis, an arthritic condition that develops between the vertebrae.

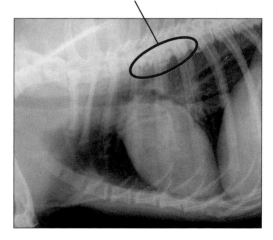

Lyme disease), resulting in a painful swollen area around the tick bite. Within a few days infection can spread through the body, eventually causing joint swellings, pain, malaise, and muscle weakness. Lyme disease is also zoonotic (transmissible to man via a bite from an infected tick) and can cause severe and dangerous flu-like illness in humans.

Affected dogs may respond to appropriate anti-borrelial antibiotics, anti-inflammatory medicines, and rest.

Tumors

Tumors can grow in locations associated with the musculoskeletal system, ranging from bone and joints to connective tissues associated with the limbs.

Symptoms

- Initially, there may be few signs of disease, but bone and joint tumors can rapidly become painful, causing lameness and reduced mobility.
- Bone tumors may also weaken affected areas of bone, predisposing them to sudden and catastrophic fractures.

Treatment Some types of chemotherapy may be appropriate in certain cases. However, bone tumors often necessitate removing affected areas of bone or amputating a limb (see page 168). In many cases, bone tumors spread rapidly to other parts of the body, and treatment may not be appropriate in dogs that have secondary tumors elsewhere in the body.

Muscle, tendon, and ligament injuries

Acute injuries may damage muscle, tendons, and ligaments, even if fractures do not occur. Affected dogs may suffer deep and painful wounds involving these important structures, or may experience over-stretch injuries that cause no skin wound but result in a swollen, damaged, painful area, where underlying structures have been pulled, stretched, or torn.

Symptoms

- Acute onset severe lameness and showing signs of pain.

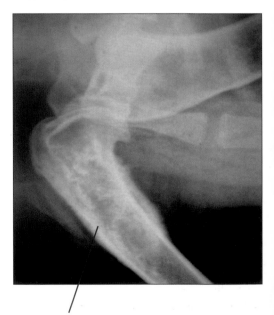

Bone tumors destroy the architecture of bone, causing severe pain and bone weakness.

- Affected limbs may be swollen or have an altered contour due to a change in the relative shape of a tissue.

Treatment Muscle injuries often heal with time, rest, and gentle anti-inflammatory medicines to relieve pain. However, some tendon or ligament injuries benefit from surgical repair to reconnect damaged tissues, otherwise long-term mobility problems may ensue.

Muscle diseases are rare, but **neurological problems** can cause muscle weakness and other conditions relating to poor muscle function.

MUSCLE ATROPHY

Loss of muscle, known as muscle atrophy, may result from damage to the nerve that supplies a particular area of muscle. A consequent severe and localized loss of muscle occurs, which can weaken and destabilize the area.

Muscle inflammation and atrophy of the muscles supplying the chewing muscles in the head is known as temporal and masseter myositis.

Symptoms

- A sudden swelling of, or loss of, muscles on the face, leading to a change in face shape, particularly in the forehead area.
- Dogs experience pain when eating and may have head pains.
- Difficulty opening the mouth fully.

Treatment High doses of steroid anti-inflammatory medicines can reduce inflammation

? What are NSAIDS

Non-steroidal anti-inflammatory medicines are a group of medicines that relieve pain and inflammation. They are used to treat a variety of conditions, including the pain and inflammation caused by arthritis.

and pain, and the underlying condition may resolve with time.

MYASTHENIA GRAVIS

This disease is characterized by generalized muscle weakness. It can occur in young, developing dogs due to congenital abnormalities, but it can also occur in older dogs.

Symptoms

- Affected animals suffer muscle weakness and tire easily. These dogs often start to exercise with enthusiasm, but quickly run out of steam and collapse (due to abnormalities in the system involved in causing muscle activity).
- Difficulty eating and swallowing (possibly).
- Dogs often suffer from **megaesophagus**, because the esophageal muscles are unable to contract effectively.

Treatment involves anti-inflammatory and pain-relieving medicines. Medicines that affect and enable neurotransmission may also be helpful.

Part 3

First aid and emergencies

A working knowledge of first aid and life-saving techniques is essential for any dog owner. It enables you to deal appropriately with any problems that arise before seeking veterinary attention and gives pets the best chance of surviving any accident or injury. While it is impossible to prepare for every eventuality, a calm and practical approach, combined with a set of basic principles, will enable you to deal appropriately with any situation that may arise.

Prevention is better than cure. Avoid accidental injuries by paying careful attention to your dog's environment and his surroundings. Keep any chemicals used in the house and yard in sealed containers that are inaccessible to your dog. Keep chocolate, medicines, and children's toys well out of canine reach. Do not allow your dog to chew stones or other foreign objects. Make sure your dog is well trained, responsive to basic commands, and does not roam. All dogs should be kept on leashes when near roads or other dangerous areas. Do not leave dogs alone in cars in the summer, even if the windows are open.

Avoid unnecessary risks where possible: give dogs safe toys and chews.

First aid

Be prepared Practice finding a heart beat and a pulse on your dog when he is well, and get used to the appearance and color of his gums, too. Practice taking his temperature and counting his breathing. Familiarity with his normal state and how to assess it will help you in an emergency situation. You might even decide to attend a pet first aid class, and it is a good idea to have a basic first aid kit on hand.

Be calm Take a deep breath before dealing with any emergency situation. Your distress will make the dog more fearful and distressed, which can contribute to an increase in pain experienced. Also, a distressed dog is more likely to respond aggressively, so be careful. A step-by-step approach allows you to concentrate on the most serious problem and not miss anything important. Call a veterinarian

FIRST AID KIT

Antiseptic solution (iodine-based or chlorhexidine) for cleaning infected skin/open wounds.

Sterile saline eyewash

Sterile, non-adherent dressing material for wounds.

WHERE TO TAKE A PULSE

Feel for a pulse on the chest just behind the elbow, or on the inner surface of the upper thigh.

Net bandages for holding a dressing in place, soft padding bandages, stretchy waterproof bandages to keep wounds clean and dry.

Flashlight. A wind-up model is ideal.

promptly and arrange an emergency appointment if necessary.

Be safe Do not put yourself in danger. A dog that is distressed and in pain behaves unpredictably, and even the sweetest-natured pooch may bite. If necessary, make a tape or gauze muzzle (see page 189) to prevent biting, so that you can concentrate on your patient without having to worry too much about your safety.

Nothing by mouth Never give an injured dog any form of medication unless you have been specifically advised to do so by a veterinarian. Although aspirin and acetaminophen are sometimes used for dogs, both can be extremely toxic to them. Do not feed injured dogs or give them water before an emergency appointment, as anesthesia may be necessary. Dogs with a full stomach can vomit and choke when anesthetized.

Thermometer. Digital models are ideal.

Magnifying glass

Scissors

Tweezers

Cotton balls

Getting
Emergency help

Few veterinarians have ambulance facilities and although medication at the site of the accident or injury may seem appropriate, usually the most important thing is to get the dog to the nearest veterinary practice as soon as possible. Be prepared to transport the injured dog there. It is a good idea to call first to check that a veterinarian is available and to explain the nature of the injuries so that all relevant equipment can be prepared.

On arrival, be ready to leave your pet for further assessment and treatment. This allows the veterinarian to concentrate on the dog's needs, rather than have to worry about the owner, too.

Collapse

Dogs may collapse for a number of reasons and the accompanying symptoms can vary.

Unconscious, no breathing/pulse

If your dog collapses and is unable to rise, first check that he can breathe and has a pulse. The following advice may be helpful (just think: A, B, C) but is no replacement for emergency veterinary attention.

Evaluate any obvious bleeding quickly, as it could rapidly affect the dog's circulation. Oozing blood is generally less serious than pumping blood (which may involve an artery). Staunch any excessive blood loss from wounds by applying pressure. This can

What if
My dog dies

If your dog collapses and there is no heart beat and pulse and no breathing, then sadly it is likely that the dog has died. If you suspect that he is dead, try checking his eye reflexes by tapping the surface of the eye with a finger. If he is alive but unconscious he will blink, but if his brain has ceased to have any activity and he is dead, he will not blink.

Is his Airway clear?

Extend the neck and try to clear any mucus or other matter from the mouth without risk of being bitten. You may need to hold his mouth open (either with your hands or a loop of material / bandage round each jaw). Remove any foreign body from within (with tweezers or pliers if possible). Gently lifting the tongue forward and to the side of the mouth helps clear the airway.

Normal vital signs

- *Temperature: normally around 101.5°F (38.6°C), but can range from 99–102.5°F (37.2–39.2°C).*
- *Pulse or heart rate: 70 (large dogs) to 140 (small dogs) beats per minute.*
- *Respiration rate: 10–30 breaths per minute.*

CARDIAC COMPRESSIONS

Apply compressions to the left side of the chest, just behind the elbow.

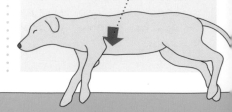

Is the dog Breathing?

Watch his sides or feel for breath at his nostrils. A normal dog's breathing rate should be 10–30 breaths per minute, but an injured dog is likely to breathe much faster. If he is not breathing, try to stimulate him by rubbing his sides. You could also try moving the hind limbs (as long as they are not injured) back and forward to try and stimulate pressure changes in the chest, which can result in breathing, or you may wish to try artificial respiration. Be aware that this is risky, even with your own dogs. Do not attempt it with unknown dogs; you could get bitten or catch a dangerous infection. Close the dog's mouth and, with your hand wrapped around it to keep it closed, make a seal over the nose with your lips (for smaller dogs, the mouth and nose). Breathe out into the dog to see if his chest rises. Release your hand pressure and move your mouth away so he can exhale. Repeat every five seconds until he is breathing normally. If you cannot see the chest rise, elevate the body so the head is lower than the chest and try again to straighten the neck and clear any mucus or debris from the mouth. Then perform artificial respiration again. Be aware: dogs can bite as they regain consciousness.

Is his Circulation working?

Check for a heartbeat on the chest wall just behind the left elbow and a pulse on the inside of the hind leg. A normal dog's heart rate is 70–140 beats per minute (depending on the size of the dog; smaller breed = faster heart rate) but an injured dog's may be much faster. Then look at the color of his gums – they should be pink. If you cannot feel a pulse, try cardiac resuscitation as follows (this is unlikely to be successful). Put the dog on his right side and find the area of the heart just behind the elbow on the left side of the chest. Apply regular compressions to this area. In big dogs you may need to use the heels of your hands to apply sufficient pressure. In small dogs you may only need one or both thumbs. The aim is to produce a downward pressure of the ribcage onto the heart to stimulate it to beat. Be careful – too much pressure can damage the ribcage.
Find a rhythm of five (big dogs) to ten (small dogs) compressions, followed by a breath into the nose or nose and mouth. Keep checking for breathing and a pulse, and stop when this has been achieved.

Below:
Check the circulation is working well and that the gums are pink and healthy.

be achieved using a tight bandage if one is available (keep putting on more layers until the blood stops coming through). Use a clean towel or a piece of material to apply pressure by hand onto a large wound if bandaging is not possible. In either case, prompt veterinary attention is important before too much blood is lost.

A pressure bandage should be removed within two to four hours at the veterinary practice, otherwise the pressure caused by the bandage can, in itself, cause serious problems.

Unconscious, breathing with a pulse

Once you have checked that the dog is breathing and that his heart and circulation are functioning, you can

How to deal with
Heat stroke

Dogs that overheat may become weak and unable to rise. They may also be breathless, hot, and have reddened mucus membranes. It is helpful to check their core temperature (see page 184). Seek urgent veterinary attention, as they may need intravenous fluid therapy. In the interim, cool them by sponging them with tepid (not cold) water.

afford to assess any further damage, although urgent veterinary attention will be needed.

- If you suspect fractures, the dog is best moved carefully on a flat board or well-supported blanket that can be used as a makeshift stretcher. If any spinal injuries are identified, it is particularly important to move dogs gently and carefully.

- If time permits – and before moving an injured dog – cover deep wounds and those that may penetrate a body cavity, preferably using a sterile dressing. However, if a foreign body is known or suspected to be in a wound, do not handle it. Leave it for the veterinarian to remove it following an assessment of the structures involved.

- Wounds due to burns should also receive prompt attention. In the interim they can be cooled with tepid water (not cold, as cold water can cause further damage).

- Even apparently shallow wounds can have serious consequences and should be seen promptly by a veterinarian.

Seizuring (convulsions)

If a dog collapses and is seizuring – meaning he is unable to stand, has limited consciousness, and may be thrashing his limbs, salivating, and maybe even passing urine and feces – first make sure that he does not hurt himself, or you.

- Ensure that his airway is clear and he is not choking on his tongue. You may need to draw the tongue forward and out to the side, but be careful not to get bitten.
- Remain calm and try to allow the dog to settle in a quiet, darkened room. In this situation, most dogs will come around within minutes, but some go into a prolonged seizure state and may need medication to stop them from seizuring.

Seek urgent veterinary advice and attention.

Weakness and inability to stand

Dogs may collapse because they are weak or unable to stand due to back or limb pain. Breathlessness and heart conditions may also cause apparent lethargy and inability to rise.

- Try to allow affected dogs to lie quietly and get their breath before attempting to help them rise. Then encourage them to get up, being ready to support them as they rise. Be careful if they are in pain, as they may behave unpredictably and could bite.
- If the back or hind legs are weak, you could help them by placing a towel or strip of fabric under the tummy and holding the

Transporting an injured dog

1 Muzzle where necessary.
2 Bandage/apply pressure to bleeding wound.
3 Ensure clear airway.
4 Stretcher the dog. Use a coat or a blanket to carry an injured dog on his side to help reduce the risk of further injury.
5 Support any injuries if possible. Try to lie the dog down on the back seat of the car and, if possible, have a helper holding him down on his side. Attempts to bandage or splint wounds often cause pain, may lead to further injury, and are usually best avoided unless severe bleeding is present which needs to be stopped.

Above: *A coat can be used as a makeshift stretcher for an injured dog.*

Collapse

A SUPPORTING SLING

A sling can be used to help a collapsed dog stand and move.

Above: *Hold the ends of a strip of fabric firmly so that it supports the hindquarters.*

ends together to help lift the dog's back end.

- If the dog is able to stand and walk with assistance, try to assess any injuries present before transporting him to the veterinarian's office by car.
- If the dog is unable to rise, use a makeshift stretcher to transport him.

How to deal with
Drowning

If drowning is suspected, try to raise the body to allow any water to drain out of the chest via the mouth and nose before trying to stimulate breathing. You can also pat the chest to encourage water to flow out, and try to clear fluid from the nostrils and mouth. Having cleared the airways and assessed the dog, perform resuscitation if necessary (see page 185). Seek emergency veterinary attention.

Elevate the hindquarters to allow water to drain out.

How to deal with
Electrocution

Electrocution can cause sudden collapse and unconsciousness and may also be associated with lack of breathing and heart activity. If suspected, DO NOT touch the affected dog until all electrical items have been identified and switched off. Then assess the dog and arrange for emergency veterinary attention while performing resuscitation if necessary.

Is the leg broken?

If a dog suddenly becomes so lame on a leg that he cannot bear weight on it, then it may be broken or severely injured. This may follow a slip while running, a fall, or a road traffic accident.

- First assess whether he is conscious and otherwise able to stand.
- Check that blood is not pouring or pumping from a wound.
- Ensure the dog is breathing normally.
- Check that it is safe to examine him in more detail. All dogs can bite when they are badly hurt; to avoid human injury it may be necessary to place a muzzle as shown.
- If the limb is hanging in an abnormal way or appears loose or floppy, it may be broken or dislocated or could have severe ligament damage. Call a veterinarian and transport the dog there as soon as possible.
- Do not offer food or water in case anesthesia is necessary. Do not give any medicines, as this may affect what the veterinarian can use at the practice to assess your dog and make him more comfortable.
- If the limb appears normal you may be able to have a good look and feel from the paw up to the body.

Be thorough and methodical; check the skin, feel the underlying tissues, and manipulate joints gently. Be careful, in case you hurt the dog. You may find a thorn in his paw that you might be able to remove, or you might find a swelling that is developing fast, indicating soft tissue injury. You may even find signs of a bite or wound that could require urgent veterinary attention.

Muzzling

1 *Take a scarf, a pair of tights, a belt, or a bandage; loop it and put one end through to make a simple knot.*

2 *Place over the dog's nose and tighten the knot under the chin.*

3 *Tie the ends behind the ears. Combined with a calm, practical approach, this technique can reduce pain, distress, and disease and even save lives.*

Right: *Applying an emergency muzzle may enable you to examine or safely move a distressed dog.*

Wounds

If a dog gets into a fight, or runs through barbed wire or over glass or a sharp stone, he may come back with a bleeding wound.

Bleeding wounds

- Check that the dog is conscious (see page 184), otherwise able to stand (see page 187), and breathing normally (see page 185).
- Rapidly staunch wounds that are pouring or pumping blood to prevent the dog from bleeding to death. First, if necessary, use a muzzle (see page 189) to prevent human injury, then apply a pressure bandage or dressing.
- If blood keeps coming through the dressing and the wound is on a lower limb, apply a tourniquet as well (see page 191).
- In the meantime, call the veterinarian and get there as quickly as possible.
- If the wound is only oozing or seeping blood, it may still be best to cover it with a dressing or bandage, pending a prompt appointment with the veterinarian. Wounds seen by a veterinarian and dealt with appropriately within a few hours (ideally less than four hours) are much more likely to heal cleanly and quickly.

The position of a wound may determine how serious it is, even if it does not appear to be bleeding severely or associated with a fracture or other serious injury.

Wounds requiring emergency attention

Wounds that can be associated with serious problems, requiring urgent or emergency attention, include injuries to the eyes, throat, chest, and abdomen. Even apparently minor abrasions in these areas can indicate deeper injuries or more serious problems, and any injuries in these locations should be assessed promptly by a veterinarian.

Eye injuries Wounds or injuries affecting the eyelids or eyes can be associated with eye damage. Internal damage to the eye can result in loss of vision, as can penetrating eye injuries, which cause a loss of pressure within the eye. Any injuries affecting the eye or tissues around it should be examined promptly by a veterinarian. If the dog is attempting to rub the eye, it may be necessary to hold or tape a sterile pad (such as those shown on page 182) over the eye, pending veterinary attention.

Applying a pressure bandage/dressing

1 If possible, first remove any obvious fragments of glass or other foreign bodies to avoid pushing them further in.
2 Press a towel or a piece of clothing directly over the wound and push hard.
3 Secure with sticky tape or strips of towel or sheet to allow further pressure to be applied. If blood keeps seeping through the dressing, do not be afraid to apply more layers a little tighter. This is a pressure bandage and is only suitable for temporary use, otherwise it may cause further damage by stopping the circulation to the underlying tissue.

Applying a tourniquet

1 Use a scarf, bandage, belt, or strip of fabric to apply pressure around the upper limb above the injury.
2 Tighten until blood flow slows and stops, but do not pull too tight, otherwise damage to the underlying skin will occur.

It is only appropriate to use a tourniquet for a brief time (ideally less than fifteen minutes), as it can cause damage to the lower limb by preventing blood circulation.

Wounds

Throat injuries can also be very serious. Typically, these are caused by foreign bodies that the dog attempts to eat (e.g., a bone) or runs into while out on a walk (e.g., a thrown stick). Injury to the back of the throat can also damage the major blood vessels and nerves in the neck, and resultant bleeding and damage to vital structures can prove fatal.

Any injuries that involve choking, coughing, excessive salivation, retching, and coughing up blood should be investigated promptly, as emergency surgery to repair damage in the throat may be necessary. Insect stings and snake bites can also cause throat swelling.

Chest injuries can involve the ribs and the lungs themselves. Although rib damage can affect breathing by causing pain during breathing, it can also contribute to lung damage. Penetration of the lungs can lead to leakage of air out of the lungs into the space around them. Air can also leak out into surrounding tissues and into the flesh under the skin. This gives the skin a "bubble wrap" feel, as pockets of air under the skin create a crackly swelling. As a result of lung collapse and leakage of air into the space around them, the lungs may be unable to inflate fully. This can contribute to breathing difficulties; seek emergency veterinary treatment.

Abdominal injuries Injuries to the abdominal wall can cause infection or damage to the peritoneum (the tissue that lines the abdomen). Bowel injuries may also result, as can liver, kidney, and bladder injuries. Peritonitis and damage to abdominal organs can be involved in life-threatening infections if not identified and treated promptly.

Applying a bandage

1 Apply a sterile dressing or clean pad to the affected areas.

2 Bandage in place, using a soft elastic bandage or tape. Work from the paw upwards to include the affected area, so that the paw does not swell due to an accumulation of fluid there.

3 Pad with a soft layer or padding bandage.

4 Locate firmly with an elastic layer. Try to bandage in a figure-eight manner if joints are involved. Cover with a breathable waterproof layer.

Flea and fly bites, as well as sand flea and mosquito bites, can cause irritation and skin disease but can also transmit a range of dangerous diseases (Lyme, heartworm). Therefore, prevention is far better than treating problems when they occur. Preventative treatments are available that kill parasites on contact with the skin and/or repel them.

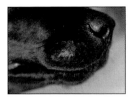

Above: A sting or bite may cause swelling, seen here on the nose.

When bites do occur they may cause a small area of inflammation, reddening, and swelling for a day or so. A more serious response may be seen in dogs that are allergic to particular bites or that sustain a bite on the face or in their airway. Bites and stings can cause rapid swelling, which can lead to difficulty breathing and may even prove fatal. Emergency treatment may be necessary. In severe cases, affected dogs may need intubation (a tube put into the airway to allow air flow) or have a tracheostomy (see page 139) to enable breathing.

Snake bites contain toxins and venom and can cause severe reactions. Seek emergency veterinary attention if you know or suspect that your dog has suffered a snake bite. Affected dogs are likely to need anti-inflammatory medicines and fluid therapy, as well as specific anti-venom, where this is available and the type of snake was identified. Many types of dangerous snake exist in different countries around the world, and local veterinarians generally hold stocks of appropriate anti-venom.

Left: Snake bites may follow curious dogs investigating long grass. Emergency treatment is required if dogs are to survive venomous bites.

Poisoning

Accidental poisoning may be witnessed or suspected if dogs have had access to rat poison, slug pellets, antifreeze, weed killer, chocolate, raisins, cleaning products, medicines, drugs, or other toxins and then appear to become ill. It may also be suspected in dogs that show signs of bleeding or bruising, breathlessness, excessive drinking, or seizuring for no known reason.

• Some poisons can cause disease following skin contact or if a dog licks himself clean after contact with a toxin. In such cases, it is important to try to prevent dogs from licking themselves. Washing with warm water or warm, slightly soapy water may also be helpful.

• If the source of poisoning is known, it is also helpful to take any details and packaging with you to the veterinarian, as this can help determine how to treat the problem.

• It may be worth obtaining advice over the telephone before the appointment. For some poisons, absorption can be limited by inducing vomiting, either by force-feeding an emetic or by an injectable emetic administered by the veterinarian. However, this can be dangerous when certain poisons are present.

• Feeding adsorbents, which help carry poisons through the body thereby reducing their absorption, can also be helpful.

• Specific antidotes are available for some poisons. Vitamin K can be given to aid recovery from anti-coagulant rodenticides.

In most cases, it is also necessary to carry out supportive treatment with medicines and fluids to support the system and treat any symptoms that occur.

How to deal with
Rodenticide poisoning

Dogs that have known access to anticoagulant rodenticides should be treated promptly and intensively. Recent ingestion can be treated by inducing emesis (vomiting) to prevent further absorption of the poison. This is best achieved using injectable emetics at the veterinarian's clinic. However, force-feeding soapy water to induce vomiting can be life-saving in an emergency.

Straining without result can be seen in dogs that cannot pass urine or feces. Sometimes it can be hard to tell what they are having trouble with, as most animals will squat and strain in a similar way if they are unable to relieve themselves.

Inability to urinate is a serious problem, as the bladder can become overstretched and may even rupture.

Back pressure can cause kidney damage and electrolyte imbalance in the body. Straining to urinate (most commonly seen in male dogs) represents an emergency and necessitates emergency veterinary attention, as it can indicate urinary blockage due to urinary diseases such as urolithiasis, swelling following an injury, or prostate swelling.

Straining to pass feces is less of an immediate emergency, although it should also receive prompt attention. Dogs may strain if they are constipated, have diarrhea, or have disease in the rectal area (prostate disease, perineal hernia).

Above: Straining to urinate can indicate bladder blockage, which is an emergency that requires prompt veterinary attention.

How to treat...
Diarrhea

On veterinary advice, affected dogs usually benefit from twenty-four hours of fasting followed by the feeding of a very bland diet (e.g., boiled, deboned chicken and rice in a one-to-two ratio) in four to six small meals daily. Seek urgent veterinary attention, especially if there are any signs of blood in the feces or if vomiting is also present.

Vomiting

Vomiting can be an indication of bowel blockage due to the presence of a foreign body (such as a toy or stone that the dog has eaten), an intestinal twist, or an intestinal blockage associated with a hernia.

Mild vomiting may constitute a problem and should be investigated promptly. However, severe, repeated vomiting, particularly where the dog cannot keep water down or where red blood or brownish partially digested blood (granular, like coffee grounds) is seen in the vomit, constitutes an emergency.

Withdraw food from affected dogs pending veterinary attention.

Hospitalization and fluid therapy may be needed to treat or prevent dehydration, in addition to specific treatment of the underlying problem.

Where surgery is needed to treat an intestinal blockage or twist, it should be prompt, as intestinal damage due to reduced blood supply can occur within two to four hours and can prove fatal.

Unsuccessful attempts at vomiting

- Attempting to vomit without success can be even more serious, particularly when other symptoms include abdominal swelling, pain, weakness, and collapse.
- Repeated unsuccessful attempts to swallow, vomit, and retch may indicate gastric torsion and volvulus.
- When the stomach swells and twists, the stomach and the spleen can lose blood supply. Severe and potentially fatal damage can occur within two to four hours.

This is an emergency situation requiring immediate veterinary attention.

Left: Partially chewed toys can be swallowed, causing an intestinal blockage, with symptoms including vomiting.

Vaginal discharge

Vaginal discharge may indicate vaginitis, a season or even the first sign of giving birth in an otherwise healthy dog. However, vaginal discharge can indicate pyometra, a potentially fatal uterine infection.

Other symptoms may include weakness, breathlessness, increased thirst, and vomiting.

Female dogs with an unusually heavy, bloody, or pus-containing discharge, or that appear to be in season at an unusual time, may have a pyometra and should be examined promptly. An emergency surgical ovariohysterectomy is generally necessary to treat pyometra.

In a pregnant female, a vaginal discharge may be associated with lack of progress during whelping and could indicate that further treatment may be necessary. Prompt treatment is needed; a Cesarean section may be needed.

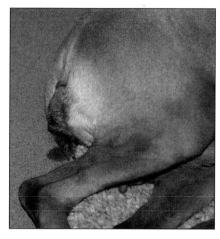

Above: A vaginal discharge containing pus is indicative of pyometra, a serious condition requiring swift attention.

PYOMETRA

In a case of pyometra, the normally small and empty non-pregnant uterus becomes distended and infected.

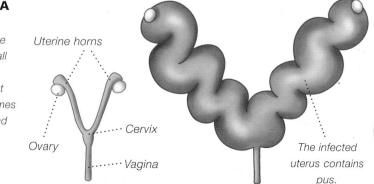

Uterine horns

Ovary

Cervix

Vagina

The infected uterus contains pus.

Vaginal Discharge

Euthanasia

Sadly, not all conditions are treatable. However well pets are cared for, they can suffer from terminal diseases or even just get to the point where old age gets the better of them. Although some sick or elderly animals do lie down and die peacefully at home, many do not do this until they have reached a stage where they are no longer comfortable. Euthanasia may become the kindest option for animals with unremitting illness or disease due to aging that cannot be controlled, where quality of life diminishes to an unacceptable level.

Although none of us wants to think of this, there can come a point where we look into the eyes of our aging or sick pet and see that the light has gone out of them and our dog's will to live has waned. Ill dogs may help us decide if they go off their food or are no longer willing to exercise. At such a time it is a good idea to check out what options are available with the veterinarian. If a decision is made to euthanize the affected animal, this can be done gently and with dignity at the veterinarian's or at the pet's home.

Euthanasia is generally carried out by a lethal injection given straight into the animal's circulation, usually into a vein in the front leg. As the drug circulates throughout the body, the dog will generally take a few deep breaths before sinking down into a lying position. Loss of brain and heart function, heralding death, follows rapidly. However, this can take longer or be more tricky in dogs with diseases that cause them to have a poor circulation, or with aggressive dogs that are difficult to handle. After death, the dog's eyes will not relax into a closed position, but they do stay open. Also, the dog's bladder and bowel may release, and for a few minutes, reflex flickery muscle movements may be seen on the sides or the limbs. The veterinarian will be able to explain anything of this nature.

Afterwards, depending on location, pets may be buried at home (although this may require permission from the local authorities) or may be transferred to a pet crematorium.

For many people, the death of a much-loved dog has the same kind of emotional effect as the death of a family member, and a natural process of grieving will follow. For some, counseling may also be necessary. Advice may also be sought concerning the psychological effect on any surviving pets, which may exhibit

signs such as withdrawal and loss of appetite when separated from their companions.

Below: *We all want our pets to live forever, but quality of life is what really counts.*

Index

Page numbers in **bold** indicate major entries, including photos; *italics* refer to captions, annotations, and panels; plain type indicates other text entries.

Credits

The publishers would like to thank the following for providing images, credited here by page number and position: (B) Bottom, (T) Top, (C) Center (BL) Bottom left, etc.

Aquarius Veterinary Centre (X-rays): 2(CB), 37(BL), 41(TL, TR), 49(BR), 70, 72, 76, 91(T), 101, 102, 126, 131(both), 135, 138(TL), 143, 159(TL), 167(both), 172(TC), 173, 177, 178

Roberta Baxter: 2(TC), 5(BR), 16(CL, BC), 18(BR), 32(BR), 39(T), 47, 48, 53(BR), 54, 55(BL), 61(TL), 62(both), 63(both), 66, 78, 91(B), 93, 95, 109, 112, 116, 119(CR), 121, 129(all), 149(both), 151(both), 156, 159(TR), 162, 163, 167 (BC, BR), 171, 176, 181(T, TC), 187, 189, 191(all), 193(T)

Jane Burton, Warren Photographic: 42, 106, 110, 111, 180

Melissa Causer: 43

Jamie David: 2(B), 9(C), 36, 117, 141

Fotolia.com: 86(B)(Valeriy Kirsanov)

Rob Gould: 18(BL), 44(both), 50, 52, 53(TL), 55(TR), 56, 58, 61(BC, BR), 67(both) 83(B), 108, 119 (TL), 128(BL), 147, 150, 155, 157, 197

iStockphoto.com: 20(Ivan Mayes), 34(Michael Pettigrew), 136(Jonathan Barnes), 181(B) and 195 (Dennis Minix), 196(Erik Lam), 199(Temelko Temelkov)

Chris Mattison: 181(CB), 193(B)

Roddy Paine ©Interpet Publishing: 30(B), 31(BL)
Pet Blood Bank UK: 125

Geoff Rogers ©Interpet Publishing: Title page, 2(T), 3, 4, 5(TL), 6, 7, 8, 9 (TR, BL, BR), 10, 11(L), 12-15, 16 (T, TC), 17, 18(T), 19 (TR), 21–29, 30(T), 31(CL), 32(TL), 33, 37(BR), 41(BR), 45, 49(TL), 59, 66(BL), 68, 73, 75, 79, 83 (T), 86(T), 89, 97, 98, 100, 127, 132, 133, 138(BR), 144, 146, 148, 154, 161, 168–169, 172(CR), 174, 182–183, 185, 195(BR)

Shutterstock.com: 113(Paul Prescott)

Neil Sutherland ©Interpet Publishing: 11(R), 19(BR all), 31(TR), 57

Ann Taggart: 103

Stuart Watkinson: 35

Publishers acknowledgments

The publishers would like to thank the following for their help during the preparation of this book:

Jean Aldridge ("Hattie"); Aquarius Veterinary Centre, Mildenhall, Suffolk ("Finlay," "Lily," "Milo" "Molly" "Roly"); Bourne Hill Kennels, Wherstead, Suffolk; Richard and Fiona Byerley ("Charlie"); Christine Farthing; Ross Fisher ("Cassie"); Christine Grantham ("Bailey"); Julia Green ("Joshua Jack" and "Megan Mollie"); Jodene **Surname** ("Coco"); Tessa Howe ("Molly"); Interpet Ltd (Mikki car harness); Sean Knights; Dave Marter ("Sophie"); Tasha Noble ("Bonnie"); Pet Blood Bank UK; Vanessa Pooley, Otley College, Suffolk; William Rogers ("Roy"); Colin and Kay Sargeant; Jenny Shotton ("Hugo"); Rachel S. Watkins, Meadow Farm Hydrotherapy, Diss, Norfolk; Ann Williams ("Beppie")

Publisher's note

The information and recommendations in this book are given without guarantee on the part of the author and publishers, who disclaim any liability with the use of this material.